THE LONG AND THE SHORT
AND THE TALL

A war play without heroics, at times comic, at others grim with the logic of war. The action takes place in the Malayan jungle early in 1942, and concerns a British patrol cut off by the Japanese advance on Singapore.

THE HEREFORD PLAYS

General Editor: E. R. Wood

Maxwell Anderson
Winterset

Robert Ardrey
Thunder Rock

Robert Bolt
A Man for All Seasons
Vivat! Vivat Regina!

Harold Brighouse
Hobson's Choice

Coxe and Chapman
Billy Budd

Barry England
Conduct Unbecoming

J. E. Flicker
Hassan

Ruth and Augustus
  Goetz
The Heiress

Nikolai Gogol
The Government
  Inspector

Willis Hall
The Long and the Short
  and the Tall

Henrik Ibsen
An Enemy of the People

Arthur Miller
The Crucible
Death of a Salesman
All My Sons
A View From the Bridge

Bill Naughton
Spring and Port Wine

André Obey
Noah

Clifford Odets
Golden Boy

J. B. Priestley
An Inspector Calls
Time and the Conways
When We Are Married
Eden End
The Linden Tree

James Saunders
Next Time I'll Sing to
  You

R. C. Sherriff
Journey's End

David Storey
In Celebration
The Changing Room

J. M. Synge
The Playboy of the
  Western World and
  Riders to the Sea

Brandon Thomas
Charley's Aunt

Peter Ustinov
Romanoff and Juliet

John Whiting
Marching Song
A Penny for a Song
The Devils

Oscar Wilde
The Importance of Being
  Earnest

Tennessee Williams
The Glass Menagerie

Willis Hall

The Long and the Short and the Tall

A PLAY IN TWO ACTS

With an Introduction and Notes by
E. R. WOOD

HEINEMANN EDUCATIONAL BOOKS
LONDON

Heinemann Educational Books Ltd
22 Bedford Square, London WC1B 3HH

LONDON   EDINBURGH   MELBOURNE   AUCKLAND
SINGAPORE   KUALA LUMPUR   NEW DELHI
IBADAN   NAIROBI   JOHANNESBURG
PORTSMOUTH (NH)   KINGSTON

ISBN 0 435 22390 9

First published 1959
This revised version first published in
The Hereford Plays 1965
Reprinted 1967, 1968 (twice), 1970, 1971, 1973, 1974, 1977,
1979, 1980, 1982, 1983, 1985, 1986 (twice)

Printed in Great Britain by
Richard Clay Ltd, Bungay, Suffolk

Contents

INTRODUCTION

WILLIS HALL was born in Leeds in 1929 and grew up there with an intimate knowledge of North-country working-class life. At an early age he wrote articles for local newspapers, and later in Singapore, where he was on military service, he regularly wrote children's radio plays and other scripts for Radio Malaya.

On returning to England in 1953 he first worked as a journalist and then became a full-time writer for BBC radio and television.

His first play for the live theatre was *The Royal Astrologer* (1957), a children's play; this was followed by *Poet and Pheasant*, a North-country comedy. Then came *The Long and the Short and the Tall*. When it was produced at the Edinburgh Festival (under the title *The Disciplines of War*) in 1958, Kenneth Tynan welcomed it as 'the most moving production of the Festival'. It was afterwards presented at the Royal Court Theatre in London, where it was a great commercial and artistic success, and later transferred to the New Theatre.

Since 1960 Willis Hall has become very widely known in collaboration with Keith Waterhouse. Their first joint success was the stage play of *Billy Liar*, based on Keith Waterhouse's novel; this ran in the West End for eighteen months. Their work is very often seen on television and they wrote the scripts of some famous films, including *Whistle Down the Wind*, *A Kind of Loving* and *Billy Liar*. Their plays for the theatre include: *Celebration*, *All Things Bright and Beautiful* and the double bill, *Squat Betty* and *The Sponge Room*. In such a collaboration it is difficult to know which partner contributes what to the finished work, but even before it began Willis

Hall had already distinguished himself by his sharp and appreciative ear for the quality of everyday speech and his satirical eye for the behaviour of ordinary people.

Themes

The Long and the Short and the Tall is a play about war and how it affects people, but it is nothing so simple as an anti-war play. Nobody in it thinks of war as a noble or glorious human activity; all are cynical in varying degrees about the way the war is run and their own rôle in it; yet there is no questioning of the causes of war and there is not a whisper of pacifism. Mitchem puts the dilemma of the soldier in the field: 'The whole lot stinks to me. So what am I supposed to do? Jack it in? Turn conshi? Leave the world to his lot?' (meaning the Japanese). He has to carry out his orders, do his duty, try to get his patrol safely back to base.

In the arguments, clashes and banter of the earlier part our attention is drawn to typical aspects of war that are disagreeable but not deeply disturbing – that military service takes men away from their homes, gives them uncongenial and futile duties, throws them together so that they get on each other's nerves, and puts them under the authority of men who enjoy shouting orders, threats and insults. Misery of this kind is remembered by millions of ex-service men. But there are compensations: in an all-male community there is relief and even fun to be had from grousing, leg-pulling, wrangling and even physical brawling.

Until the Japanese soldier comes into the play, none of the men except Mitchem and Johnstone has any experience of the work for which war is organized – killing. The tone until then is mainly comic. When Johnstone grabs the intruder and yells at one after another to stick a bayonet into him, the play confronts us with the reality of war – but only for a moment: Mitchem says he wants the prisoner alive, and the tension is relaxed. It is only later, when the prisoner has developed into a human being, a soldier like themselves, with a wife and kids at home, that the real challenge comes. When they learn that they are cut off by Japanese forces, with only a slender chance of getting back to base, military sense demands that they kill the prisoner, whatever the Geneva Convention says. Everybody is put to the test. For Mitchem, the justification is 'It's a war'; for Johnstone (who likes killing) 'he's a bloody Nip!'; others agree or want to shirk responsibility: only Bamforth, who was ready enough to kill him in the heat before he knew him as a human being, now calls it murder. From the point of view of the logic of war, Mitchem is right: Bamforth, the last person to take a high moral tone, thinks and feels not as a soldier but as a man.

The author has said that the play is about human dignity. War has little room for human dignity. The soldier's task is easier if he can regard his enemy as merely a 'bloody Nip', a 'wog' – a thing to be despised or hated, not to be thought of as a human being. This aspect of war is so obvious that it is hardly worth stating in words: what the play does is bring it home to us in terms of flesh and blood.

It should be clear in any case that the author is not preaching a doctrine, telling us how men should act, offering a solution of a problem. On the contrary, he belongs to the contemporary movement in the theatre, where we are confronted with disturbing questions to which there is no easy answer. Of course we find ourselves on Bamforth's side, but we can understand Mitchem and sympathize in some degree with the others. Above all we feel for the prisoner, who is mute and bewildered throughout.

Characters

The characters are first seen on the level of easily recognizable types. We have a Scot, a Welshman, a Tynesider, a Cockney, each with characteristics generally supposed to belong to their races; or, classifying in a different way, we have a typical army sergeant, a raw recruit who is both cowardly and incompetent, a 'barrack-room lawyer', and every soldier's image of the sadistic corporal. We think we know them at once and how we shall react to each. The characterization is then deepened by the author, so that we see other aspects: we hear about Evans's girl in Cardiff, about Smith's home life on the council estate, about Whitaker's touching romance in Catterick; we find that Macleish is quick to take offence, that he cannot stand ragging about being a Scot or about his promotion to lance-corporal, and that he is deeply worried about his brother. In Bamforth we see some of the qualities that made Jimmy Porter so compelling a stage character in *Look Back in Anger* – an arrogant emancipation from conventional ideas about class, authority, love and generally the world around us, uninhibited eloquence in uttering his contempt, a capacity for real friendship hidden under scoffing and brawling, and the power to evoke from the audience a mixed response, liking mingled with dislike. In the scrapping with Evans there is no harm intended (it is like the good-natured sparring of schoolboys), but the readiness to fight Johnstone is earnest and primitive, for in the slums where he has grown up a male has to stand up for himself or be dominated by bullies. This he is only too eager to do. There is nothing in the least sentimental in his defence of the Japanese prisoner; he begins by treating him as if he were some sub-human creature to be taught tricks and he continues to regard him as a sort of mascot; his revulsion from the Johnstone-Mitchem line comes from a spontaneous sense of justice and human decency, but there is nothing self-consciously noble or humanitarian in his stand, which is accompanied throughout by coarse insults to those who oppose or desert him.

With the exception of Johnstone all the characters evoke some sympathy. Even the contemptible Whitaker has his moment when the audience is moved by the story of his meetings with Mary Pearson:

So we'd just walk along by the side of the river, like. Up as far as
the bridge. Happen sit down and watch them playing bowls. Sit
for ten minutes or so, get up and walk back. . . . I never had much
money – only my bus fare there and back sometimes . . .

Smith is the only member of the patrol who shows any
sympathy with Whitaker, and his gentleness towards him adds
much to the quiet effectiveness of this scene. He himself has a
similar passage when he talks of his garden: 'Made a sort of a
bit of a lawn of it. Sit out on Sundays on it after dinner. Me
and the missis. Saturday afternoon sometimes – when there
was football on the wireless.' The simplicity of their language
echoes the simplicity of their lives. Such people ask for nothing
very grand to make them happy – or so it seems as they look
back from the Malayan jungle on what they have lost.

So far the development of character has consisted in letting
each reveal more of his past and in showing how they react to
each other. Now the grim events of the war situation test their
mettle and reveal new strengths and weaknesses. On Mitchem
falls the duty to make decisions. He has no illusions about the
glory and heroism of the soldier's life. 'The trouble is with
war – a lot of it's like this – too much.' He tells Macleish: 'If
this war shapes the way I think it will, you'll grow up, lad, in
next to no time. Before this month is out you'll do a dozen
jobs like this (i.e. killing the prisoner) before you have your
breakfast.' They learn soon what war means, but before they
have the chance to 'grow up' they are all dead except Johnstone.
When put to the test only Bamforth grows in stature: in the
clash with Mitchem all the others let him down.

Johnstone is different from the rest in that our sympathy
for him is never aroused, and even Mitchem does not like
him. Yet his attitude is the logic of war; he hates his enemy
violently and passionately. His final surrender, too, is logical.
In a note on this the author has written:*

* *Amateur Stage*, July 1960.

> This should not be accepted as any sign of cowardice. He is, in fact, a soldier who has done all that he can in his fight against the enemy and now, as a wounded man, is surrendering and therefore making himself a liability to the enemy – will no doubt later attempt to escape – rather than allow himself to be killed uselessly.

If the Japanese follow Johnstone's ideas about how to treat prisoners, he will not be a liability for long.

The most important character in the play, though he is not given a word of dialogue, is the Japanese prisoner. He is a simple soldier (his nationality is irrelevant) caught up in a situation he does not understand. His rôle in the play is to pose by his mere presence a simple and yet crucial question about war. The military virtues seem noble enough, military necessity only too compelling, until war is seen as men killing men.

Theatrical Qualities

Among the reasons for the immediate and lasting success of this play on the stage are the dramatic clashes between members of the patrol, set against the increasing menace to them all from outside. Everyone knows that one essential ingredient of drama is conflict. Conflict between Bamforth and Johnstone enlivens the opening moments. Tension is then relaxed, and for half an hour or so the tone is mainly comic. The purpose of this passage is to present to us the individuals in the patrol and to convey the barrack-room atmosphere in this jungle hut, so far free from intimations of disaster. Bamforth is involved in wrangles in which there is no malice, until a futile row with Macleish blows up into a real threat to the peace, and this conflict shifts its ground and sharpens further when Mitchem and Johnstone come in.

Tension is again relaxed, until the intrusion of a Japanese voice on the radio alerts everyone with its implications of unexpected danger outside the hut. Still greater dramatic excitement comes when a Japanese soldier is seen approaching and this mounts to a climax as he comes in and is grabbed by Johnstone. Then there is a gradual lowering of the theatrical temperature. Interest is focused on the prisoner and there is at first more laughter than tension, until a clash between Johnstone and Bamforth becomes ugly. This is interrupted by news of the Japanese having broken through, and the menace from outside builds up to the end of the act, when the Japanese voice on the radio taunts and threatens them all.

The foregoing outline shows how dramatic tension rises throughout the first act, but in a series of climaxes, each followed by relief, until the last. The same skill in construction is to be seen in the second act, but there is an important difference – that there is more tension, and the quieter passages are more often touching than comic. This act leads up to the final clash between Bamforth and Mitchem, with its tremendous climax when Whitaker shoots the prisoner. After a moment to take in the situation, and the final spurt of anger in which Mitchem strikes Bamforth, we move on to the last climax – the firing outside that wipes out the patrol except for Johnstone, whose surrender ends the play.

The grim story is excitingly told, the characters are progressively explored, questions about war and humanity are thrust at us to disturb our complacency, all without any departure from the tradition of naturalistic drama. The illusion that we are watching real men in a real situation, the claustrophobic sense of being in a small hut with a hostile jungle all around, the boredom, the badinage, the tension and the violence: all this can be intensely real on the stage. It does not happen by chance: it is achieved by expert craftsmanship and a sure instinct for what is effective in a theatre.

The language

The language of the play contributes much to our feeling that these are real soldiers of today. The theatre has suffered in the past from what J. B. Priestley once called 'the flavourless patter of modern realistic dialogue'. It seemed that if the characters talked as real people did, their language must be flat, cliché-ridden, devitalized. This was always more true of respectable middle-class speech than of provincial dialects or low-life slang, and the drama has gained in the last decade from its preoccupation with people whose talk is non-literary and often uncouth. Willis Hall has here assembled from a variety of sources a language that is full of flavour and vitality. The Scot, the Welshman, the Tynesider and the Cockney each bring peculiarities of provincial speech, which enrich the dialogue and reinforce regional features of temperament. But more important is the use of slang of various kinds, especially service slang, which has marked advantages for stage purposes.

First, its authenticity: the men really talk like soldiers, only more so. Service language gives the soldier a sense of belonging to a closed circle. A young recruit will quickly learn to cover up his civilian habits of speech by absorbing a new vocabulary. Quite ordinary needs like sleep, smoke, cigarette, food and girl have to be translated into slang equivalents, such as *kip*, *drag*, *nub*, *connor* and *bint*. Often slang is the soldier's means of escape from anything solemn, sentimental, pompous or official. So your comrades are your *muckers*, your unit is your *mob*, insisting on correct military procedure is *coming it regimental*. Slang is an inexact language. The same expression may mean many different things and none of them clearly defined.* Compared with standard English it is madly unstable; the newly-coined phrase of one decade becomes the jaded old

---

* There may be a positive advantage in not defining precisely what is meant. Expressions concerning violence or insubordination avoid the language in which an official report might be made or a charge might be framed. For example, if you *come it on* with one of your *mob* he may *sort you out* and *stick you one on*, but if you were to *carve him up* or *knock him off* you would be *for the high jump – and no messing*. This may be difficult to translate into a clear statement of what happened or may happen.

cliché of the next or it spreads and slips in meaning, or even mercifully dies out. It would not do for expressing subtle or profound thought or emotion; it is more effective for disparaging than for inspiring or encouraging; but it suits exactly the attitudes and atmosphere of Sergeant Mitchem and his men.

Though slang is always changing, and the soldier must keep up to date, it is surprising how many vestiges remain of earlier wars and long-forgotten service in India or the Middle East. No soldier of the last war had known Fred Karno, a comedian of the pre-1914 music-hall, yet the phrase *Fred Karno's mob* survives as an echo of a soldier song of a previous generation. *Bungy, connor, gillo, wallah, bramah, doolally* and *Blighty* are old slang from British India, and *shufti* and *bint* come from Arabic.

Just as there is an odd satisfaction for soldiers in talking a language of their own, so in the theatre an audience enjoys being brought into the exclusive group. Moreover, at the time when the play was first presented, millions of men and women had spent some time in the services, and they found themselves back in a familiar atmosphere.

An audience can enjoy the shock of hearing language spoken in public that is not decorous or even respectable, but which has energy. Sometimes it has a brutal vividness, as, for example, when Mitchem speaks of how there could have been 'seven men with their tripes on the floor'.

The degree to which slang is shocking to the fastidious partly depends on its origins. Some slang is intentionally coarse, being pre-occupied with sex or other taboos of polite conversation. So talk which is acceptable in the barrack-room or a men's bar-parlour may sound gross to a mixed audience in a theatre, though not everybody there will know what the 'rude' words mean. Again, some of our slang originates in low life and even in the semi-secret codes of criminals. Often these sources are now forgotten, but there remains a taint of the underworld. A good deal of the slang used in this play is

Cockney in origin – a London speech which is far remote from that of Mayfair or Kensington.

An oddity of language which is not always recognized is the phenomenon of rhyming slang. Thus the word *bonce* is familiar in jocular slang, while its rhyming source *sconce* has fallen out of common use. *Half-inch* is an obvious rhyming pair with *pinch*; but sometimes the slang expression is incomplete and the lost element has to be restored to form the rhyme originally intended. For example, a *butcher's* means a *look* because it was once a *butcher's hook*; when you are told to *use your loaf*, it is your *loaf of bread* that rhymes with *head*; if you are called a *creamer*, it means you are a *mug* because it rhymes with *cream-jug*.

It will be seen from the above that rhyming slang may provide a euphemism for a taboo word or a disguise for criminal activities, or it may have a touch of ironic humour; but often it seems pointless and even silly.* But living language is prone to needless proliferation.

Catch-phrases from the music-halls are perpetuated in slang after the context is forgotten. Bamforth uses such an obsolete catch-phrase when he talks of 'sorting out the judies from Land's End to *how's your father*'. The meaning conveyed is intentionally vague, but there is an intangible note of irreverence.

Although slang is often impoverished language, full of imprecise words endlessly repeated to avoid the effort needed to express exactly what is meant, the general effect in such a play as this is one of toughness and energy. Phrases like *so fast your feet won't touch the ground, up the creek without a paddle* or *have your guts for garters* become clichés by over-use, but on first hearing they have an expressiveness that makes more formal English seem insipid. You may not know the precise connotation of oft-repeated words of abuse like *burk*,

---

* There may be some wry humour in *trouble and strife* instead of *wife*, but there is little point in *skin and blister* for *sister*.

get, creep or *slob,* but they all sound vigorously insulting. Language like this (at least when it is fresh) sounds virile and free from the nice virtues.

In the post-war world slang has come to express a widespread attitude of mind. The young of today have a sharp ear for anything that sounds *wet* or *corny*; they like a person to be natural and spontaneous, not dignified or *stuffy*. On a historic occasion when a great mountaineer came down the ice-slopes from climbing the highest mountain in the world, his first words to the leader of the expedition were not 'We have a tale to tell that will stir the heart of every Briton', but 'We've knocked the bastard off!' The tone of his report, which would have shocked our grandparents, seems right today.

Contrast with Journey's End

It is fascinating to compare *The Long and the Short and the Tall* (1958) with R. C. Sherriff's classic of the First World War, *Journey's End* (1928). But more significant than the resemblances are the differences. In the thirty years between the two plays there has been a radical change in the attitude to war, not, perhaps, of soldiers in the field, but of theatre audiences. This is partly a matter of class-consciousness. In *Journey's End* it is taken for granted that the men who count are from the public school class: the rest may be good fellows in their way, but they are regarded with an indulgent smile; they drop their aitches and have provincial accents. There is no class-consciousness in *The Long and the Short and the Tall*; as the title hints, the characters are just men.

In the First World War it would have been usual for a boy like Raleigh to come fresh from his public school to hold commissioned rank in France, and it would have seemed quite natural to a theatre audience of the late 'twenties that he should bring to the trenches the games-obsession which was thought to be the foundation of success on the battlefield. So when Osborne says of Captain Stanhope, 'He's a splendid chap,' young Raleigh replies, 'Isn't he? He was skipper of Rugger at Barford, and kept wicket for the eleven. A jolly good bat, too.'

It may be amusing to speculate on what Bamforth would have said to that. We know exactly what he would have said to Raleigh's exclamation: 'How topping if we both get the M.C.!' But Bamforth does not set out to be a good soldier. Sergeant Mitchem *is* a good soldier, but even he is cynical about medals: 'The army's full of square-head yobs who keep their brains between their legs. Blokes who do their nuts for fifteen seconds and cop a decoration, cheer boys cheer, Rule Britannia and death before dishonour.'

Sergeant Mitchem has problems in keeping his men to their duty in war: Captain Stanhope also has to stiffen a coward who would let the side down. His approach would not do in Mitchem's unit:

> If you went – and left Osborne and Trotter and Raleigh and all those men up there to do your work – could you ever look a man straight in the face again – in all your life? You may be wounded. Then you can go home and feel proud – and if you're killed you . . . won't have to stand this hell any more. . . . But you're still alive – with a straight fighting chance of coming through. Take the chance, old chap, and stand in with Osborne and Trotter and Raleigh. Don't you think it worth standing in with men like that? - when you know that they all feel like you do – in their hearts – and just go on sticking it because they know it's the only decent thing a man can do?

Mitchem would have understood Stanhope's situation and needs, but the style now seems to belong to the housemaster's or prefect's study of a past generation.

Of course, the language of *Journey's End*, so much less vigorous than that of *The Long and the Short and the Tall*, is true to its period. The rather vapid slang is out of date now, but many of the phrases such as 'I'd like to awfully, old man', 'You'll put up a good show', 'strong, keen chaps', were then – and still are – characteristic of the officer class. It is a disadvantage of writing plays about middle-class Englishmen that such people, especially in emotional stress, take refuge in stereotyped speech which inhibits real self-expression. There is a moment in *Journey's End* when the author comes near to making an explicit statement, through his characters, on trench warfare. Osborne describes how on one occasion the Germans chivalrously allowed and encouraged the British to recover a wounded man from No Man's Land between the trenches:

> OSBORNE: A big German officer stood up in their trenches and called out 'Carry him!' – and our fellows stood up and carried the man back, and the German officer fired some lights for them to see by.
> RALEIGH: How topping!
> OSBORNE: Next day we blew each other's trenches to blazes.
> RALEIGH: It all seems rather – *silly*, doesn't it?
> OSBORNE: It does, rather.

The inadequacy of the language is intentional. Among such Englishmen understatement is a virtue.

Moreover, the theatre audience of the time preferred a cool tone. They were ready to be moved by the play, but in reason. The picture of war must not be too harshly unsettling. What happens may be tragic, but what is said should be in good taste. Raleigh, with a lump of a shell in his back, says in gasps: 'So – damn – silly – getting hit,' asks for water, then, 'Could we have a light? It's – it's so frightfully dark and cold' and dies with 'something between a sob and a moan'. For Mitchem, the death of a new recruit is uglier: 'Few weeks after that and he's on his back with his feet in the air and a hole as big as your fist in his belly. And he's nothing.'

The distribution and effect of the comedy in the two plays is different. In *The Long and the Short and the Tall* most of the comedy is disillusioned, bitter, tough. In *Journey's End* it serves to cushion the audience from body blows. Laughter is introduced from time to time to ensure that the audience is not made too uncomfortable. It shows that our brave lads do not take things too tragically. When Trotter is confronted with soup without pepper, he makes a fuss and says, 'War's bad enough with pepper, but war without pepper – it's – it's bloody awful!' The laughter that greets this truth keeps things in proportion. While our troops can joke in the face of death we can call on them to stick it (in Stanhope's sense, of course, not Bamforth's). There is plenty of laughter in *The Long and the Short and the Tall*, but most of it comes before the war situation really hits the patrol, and none of it is cosy.

Journey's End has enough virtues to have kept it alive for a third of a century: it has credible characters, poignant and dramatic situations, faultless technique. If it suffers by comparison with *The Long and the Short and the Tall*, that is because there have been such changes in our society, and in the theatre, since its time.

THE LONG AND THE SHORT
AND THE TALL

They say there's a troopship just leaving Bombay,
Bound for Old Blighty shore,
Heavily-laden with time-expired men,
Bound for the land they adore.
There's many a soldier just finishing his time,
There's many a twirp signing on,
You'll get no promotion this side of the ocean,
So cheer up, my lads, bless 'em all!

Bless 'em all! Bless 'em all!
The long and the short and the tall;
Bless all the sergeants and W.O.1s,
Bless all the corp'rals and their blinkin' sons,
'Cos we're saying goodbye to them all,
As back to their billets they crawl,
You'll get no promotion this side of the ocean,
So cheer up, my lads, bless 'em all!

They say, if you work hard you'll get better pay,
We've heard it all before,
Clean up your buttons and polish your boots,
Scrub out the barrack-room floor.
There's many a rookie has taken it in,
Hook line and sinker an' all,
You'll get no promotion this side of the ocean,
So cheer up, my lads, bless 'em all!

   Bless 'em all! *etc.*

They say that the Sergeant's a very nice chap,
Oh! What a tale to tell!
Ask him for leave on a Saturday night
He'll pay your fare home as well.
There's many a soldier has blighted his life,
Thro' writing rude words on the wall,
You'll get no promotion this side of the ocean,
So cheer up, my lads, bless 'em all!

   Bless 'em all! *etc.*

They say that the Corp'ral will help you along,
Oh! What an awful crime,
Lend him your razor to clean up his chin,
He'll bring it back every time.
There's many a rookie has fell in the mud,
Thro' leaving his horse in the stall,
You'll get no promotion this side of the ocean,
So cheer up, my lads, bless 'em all!

   Bless 'em all! *etc.*

Nobody knows what a twirp you've been,
So cheer up, my lads, bless 'em all!

The Long and the Short and the Tall was first produced at the Nottingham Playhouse on 1 September 1958; it was also presented by the Oxford Theatre Group on the 'Fringe' of the 1958 Edinburgh Festival. It was directed by Peter Dews.

The play was first produced in London on 7 January 1959 at the Royal Court Theatre, then transferred to the New Theatre on 8 April 1959. It was presented by the English Stage Company in association with Oscar Lewenstein and Wolf Mankowitz, with the following cast:

465 SERGEANT MITCHEM, R	Robert Shaw
839 CORPORAL JOHNSTONE, E.	Edward Judd
594 L/CORPORAL MACLEISH, A. J.	Ronald Fraser
632 PRIVATE WHITAKER, S.	David Andrews
777 PRIVATE EVANS, T. E.	Alfred Lynch
877 PRIVATE BAMFORTH, C.	Peter O'Toole
611 PRIVATE SMITH, P.	Bryan Pringle
A JAPANESE SOLDIER	Kenji Takaki

The play directed by LINDSAY ANDERSON
with décor by ALAN TAGG

CHARACTERS

465 SERGEANT MITCHEM, R.
839 CORPORAL JOHNSTONE, E.
594 L/CORPORAL MACLEISH, A. J.
632 PRIVATE WHITAKER, S.
777 PRIVATE EVANS, T. E.
877 PRIVATE BAMFORTH, C.
611 PRIVATE SMITH, P.
A JAPANESE SOLDIER

The action of the play takes place in the Malayan jungle during the Japanese advance on Singapore, early in 1942.

ACT ONE

Time: Late afternoon.

*The curtain rises on the wooden-walled, palm-thatched, dingy
interior of a deserted store-hut in the Malayan jungle. The hut
is set back a few hundred yards from a tin mine which is now
deserted. There is a door in the rear wall with windows on either
side looking out on to the veranda and jungle beyond. The hut
has been stripped of everything of any value by the mine-workers
before they fled – all that remains is a rickety table and two chairs,
Centre Stage, and a form, Right. We hear a short burst of heavy
gunfire in the distance – and then silence. A pause and then we
hear the chirruping of crickets and the song of a bird in the jungle.
A figure appears at the Left Hand window, looks cautiously inside
and ducks away. A moment later the door is kicked open and
JOHNSTONE stands framed in the doorway, holding a sten at his
hip. When the door was kicked open the crickets and the bird
ceased their song. JOHNSTONE glances around the room and,
finding it unoccupied, makes a hand signal from the veranda.
JOHNSTONE returns into the room and is joined a few seconds
later by MITCHEM, who also carries a sten.*

JOHNSTONE (*shifts his hat to the back of his head and places his
sten on the table*): All Clear. Stinks like something's dead.

MITCHEM (*placing his sten beside Johnstone's*): It'll do. To be
going on with. (*He crosses to the door and motions to the rest
of the patrol.*) Come on, then! Let's have you! . . . Move it!
Move!

*One by one the members of the patrol double into the room.
With the exception of* WHITAKER, *who carries the radio
transmitter/receiver on his back, the men are armed with rifles.*

1

SMITH *carries* WHITAKER's *rifle. They are tired and dishevelled.*

JOHNSTONE: Move yourselves! Gillo! Lacas! Lacas!

As the last member of the patrol enters the room MITCHEM *slams the door. The men stack their rifles in a corner of the hut and sit gratefully on the table.* WHITAKER *takes off the 'set' and sets it up on the table.* BAMFORTH *shrugs off his pack, places it as a pillow on the form, and makes himself comfortable.*

JOHNSTONE: How long we here for?

MITCHEM (*glances at his watch*): Half an hour or so, and then we'll push off back. Better mount a guard. Two men on stag. Fifteen minute shifts.

JOHNSTONE: Right . . . (*He notices* BAMFORTH *who is now fully stretched out.*) Bamforth! . . . Bamforth!

BAMFORTH (*raises himself with studied unconcern*): You want me, Corp?

JOHNSTONE: Get on your feet, lad!

BAMFORTH: What's up?

JOHNSTONE: I said 'move'! (BAMFORTH *pulls himself slowly to his feet.*) You think you're on your holidays? Get your pack on!

BAMFORTH: You going to inspect us, Corp?

JOHNSTONE: Don't give me any of your mouth. Get your pack on! Smartish! Next time you keep it on till you hear different.

BAMFORTH (*heaves his pack on to one shoulder*): All right! O.K. All right.

JOHNSTONE: Right on!

BAMFORTH *glances across at* MITCHEM.

MITCHEM: You heard what he said.

BAMFORTH (*struggles the pack on to both shoulders. He speaks under his breath*): Nit!

There is a pause. JOHNSTONE *crosses to face* BAMFORTH.

JOHNSTONE: What was that?

BAMFORTH: Me. I only coughed.

MITCHEM: O.K., Bamforth. Just watch it, son.

JOHNSTONE: Too true, lad. Watch it. Watch it careful. I've had my bellyfull of you this time out. You watch your step. Put one foot wrong. Just one. I'll have you in the nick so fast your feet won't touch the ground. Just you move out of line, that's all.

BAMFORTH: You threatening me, Corp?

JOHNSTONE: I'm warning you!

BAMFORTH: I got witnesses!

JOHNSTONE: You'll have six months. The lot. I'll see to that, Bamforth. I'll have your guts. One foot wrong, as sure as God I'll have your guts.

BAMFORTH: Try. Try it on for size.

MITCHEM (*crosses to intervene*): Right. Pack it in. That's both of you. (BAMFORTH *turns away from* JOHNSTONE.) I want two men for guard. First stag. Two volunteers . . . Come on, come on!

SMITH (*pulls himself to his feet*): First or second – what's the odds . . .

MACLEISH (*follows suit*): It's all the same to me.

MITCHEM: Better stay inside. Don't show yourselves. Cover the front. If anything's to come it's coming from out there. (MACLEISH *and* SMITH *take up their rifles and move across to cover the windows.*) How's the set?

WHITAKER (*looks up from tuning in the radio*): It's dead. Still dis. U/s. Can't get a peep. I think the battery's giving up. Conking out.

BAMFORTH: Now he tells us! Signals! Flipping signallers – I've shot 'em. Talk about the creek without a paddle.

MITCHEM: You got any suggestions, Bamforth . . .

BAMFORTH: Only offering opinions.

MITCHEM: Well don't! Don't bother. If we want opinions from you we'll ask for them. From now on keep them to yourself. Now, pay attention. All of you. We're sticking here for half an hour at the most. After that we're . . . heading back for camp. (*A murmur of relief from the men.*) Anybody any questions?

EVANS: Can we have a drag, Sarge?

MITCHEM: Yeh. Smoke if you want. You can get the humpy off your backs. Get what rest you can. Your best bet is to grab some kip. It's a long way back. Another thing, you'd better save your grub. I make it we'll get back before tomorrow night – but just in case we don't, go steady on the compo packs. O.K.? (*There is a murmur of agreement from the men.*) I want to have a sortie round. Outside. See how we're fixed. Check up. Fancy a trot, Johnno?

JOHNSTONE: Suits me.

The patrol remove their packs and place them on the floor.
MITCHEM *and* JOHNSTONE *pick up and check their stens.*

MITCHEM: Keep at it on the set, Sammy son. Have another shot at getting through.

WHITAKER (*puts on headphones*): Right, Sarge. Don't think it's going to do much good.

MITCHEM: Keep bashing. Mac!

MACLEISH (*turns from window*): Aye?

MITCHEM: We're having a stroll as far as the road. You're i/c. We won't be long. As far as we know there's nothing in the area for miles – but if anything crops up – I mean, if you should see anything – don't shoot. Unless you've got to. Right?

MACLEISH: Fair enough.

MITCHEM: Ready, Johnno? (JOHNSTONE *nods and follows* MITCHEM *to the door.*) And keep your voices down, the lot of you.

JOHNSTONE: Bamforth! That includes you!

BAMFORTH (*who has been delving into his pack*): I heard!

MITCHEM: Come on.

MITCHEM *opens the door and exits, followed by* JOHNSTONE. *We see them move past window and disappear down the veranda steps.*

BAMFORTH (*throwing down his pack in disgust*): The creep. The stupid nit!

EVANS: Johnno's got it in for you, boyo. He'll have your guts for garters yet. He's after you. Chases you round from haircut to breakfast time.

BAMFORTH: Flipping toe-rag! He wants carving up. It's time that nit got sorted out. When this lot's over – when I get back to civvy street – I only want to meet him once. In town. That's all. Just once. Will someone see me now and hear my prayers. If I could come across him once without them tapes to come it on! I'll smash his face.

EVANS: Go on, man! He's twice the size of you! You wouldn't stand a chance, tapes or no tapes.

BAMFORTH: What do you know about scrapping? That's how you want them when you're putting in the nut. Up there. Bigger than yourself. And then you wham 'em – thump across the eyes. Straight across the eyes and then the knee and finish with the boot. All over. Send for the cleaners.

EVANS: You wouldn't fight like that, Bammo?

BAMFORTH: You want to lay me odds? I'll take fives on that. What do you know about it, you ugly foreigner? Get back to Wales, you Cardiff creep. Only good for digging coal and singing hymns, your crummy lot.

EVANS: Shows how much you know, boy. You want to see some real fighting, Bammo, you go to Cardiff on a Saturday night. Round the docks. Outside the boozers. More fights in one night than you've had hot dinners.

BAMFORTH: Country stuff, son. Country stuff. You haven't got the first idea. You ever want to see a bloke carved up? Proper? So his missis thinks he's someone else? You hand that job to London boys.

SMITH (*glancing over his shoulder from the window*): Why don't you jack it in?

BAMFORTH: What's that?

SMITH: You heard. I said, 'give it a rest'.

BAMFORTH: I never heard your name and number in this conversation.

SMITH: I'm just telling you, that's all. I've had about enough. Bloody southerners shouting the odds. Always shouting the odds. You're like the rest. One look at a barmaid and you're on the floor.

EVANS: That's what barmaids are for, Smudge.

BAMFORTH: Good old Taff! And I always thought you were a presbyterian.

EVANS: Strict Chapel. Every Sunday.

BAMFORTH: Sunday's his day off. When he leaves the milkmaid alone. Tuesdays and Wednesdays he's going steady with a Eistedfodd.

SMITH: Come again?

BAMFORTH: One of them bints in a long black hat and bits of lace. Always singing songs. Every time you go to the pictures you see them on the news. Singing songs and playing harps and that. Hymns. Like being in church only it's outside. Dodgy move – so they can whip them up the mountainside for half an hour afterwards. Very crafty boys, these Taffs. You've got to hand it to them.

EVANS: Go on, man!

BAMFORTH: Straight up. It's straight up, son. Got any fags, have you, Taff?

EVANS: I thought you must be after something.

    EVANS *takes a packet of cigarettes from his trouser pocket and offers one to* BAMFORTH *as he crosses towards him.* BAMFORTH *takes the cigarette.*

BAMFORTH: So what? As long as it's only your fags I'm after, you've no need to worry, have you, son? My name's not Johnno.

MACLEISH (*turning at window*): Bamforth, why don't you pack it in! We've heard about enough from you.

BAMFORTH: Silence in court! Acting Unpaid Lance Corporal Macleish is just about to pull his rank! Don't it make you sick! Doesn't it make you want to spew, eh? Sew a bit of tape on their arms and all at once they talk like someone else. What's the matter, Mac? You chasing your second stripe already?

MACLEISH: Are you looking for trouble, Bamforth? Because if you are you can have it, and no messing.

BAMFORTH: Ah, shut up, you Scotch haggis! Dry up, boy! It's not your fault. All Corps are bastards, we all know that.

MACLEISH: Watch your mouth! As far as I'm concerned the tape's not worth it. Just remember that. As far as I'm concerned I'll jack the tape tomorrow to drop you one on. And that's a promise, Bamforth.

BAMFORTH: Go stuff your tape.

EVANS *lights his cigarette behind dialogue.*

MACLEISH: So just watch your mouth.

BAMFORTH: Aw, come off it, son. Where I come from it's just a name.

MACLEISH: It so happens I don't like it.

SMITH: Drop it, Mac. He didn't mean no harm.

MACLEISH: I'm willing to accept his apology.

BAMFORTH: So what's the argument about? Here, Taffy, give us a touch, boy.

EVANS (*hands cigarette to* BAMFORTH *who lights his own and passes it back*): I don't see, Mac, what you got to complain about. Bammo's only having you on. Before you got that tape you moaned about Johnno just as much as the rest of us. More, perhaps.

SMITH: Just let it drop, Taff, eh?

MACLEISH: It so happens that I accepted the rank of Lance Corporal. Having accepted the rank, and the responsibility that goes with it, I feel it's my duty to back up my fellow N.C.O.s. And that decision is regardless of any personal prejudices I might hold.

BAMFORTH: King's Regulations, Chapter Three, Verse

Seventeen. The congregation will rise and sing the hymn that's hanging up behind the door of the bog.

MACLEISH: You're just a head case, Bamforth. You're a nutter. Round the bend.

BAMFORTH (*jumping up on chair*): With the inspired help of our dear friend and member, Fanny Whitaker, who will accompany the choir on her famous five-valve organ. All together, please! The chorus girl's lament! (*Sings.*)

My husband's a corporal, a corporal, a corporal,
A very fine corporal is he!
All day he knocks men about, knocks men about, knocks men about,
At night he comes home and knocks me!

EVANS *joins* BAMFORTH *in the chorus.*

Singing Hey-jig-a-jig, cook a little pig, follow the band.
Follow the band all the way!
Singing Hey-jig-a-jig, cook a little pig, follow the band
Follow the band all the way!

WHITAKER (*glances up from tuning set*): Pack it in, Bamforth.

BAMFORTH (*unheeding and improvising*): Order if you please, Second verse. (*Sings.*)

Oh, as soon as this lot's through, I'll be off to Waterloo,
And I'll be out on the town right away,
And you might as well clear off
'Cause things get bloody tough
When Bammo's on the town every day.

EVANS *joins* BAMFORTH *again in the chorus.*

Singing Hey-jig-a-jig, cook a little pig, follow the band.
Follow the band all the way!
Singing Hey-jig-a-jig . . .

WHITAKER (*rising, angrily*): Will you pack it in!

BAMFORTH (*jumps to floor*): Hello! Our little blue-eyed signaller doing his nut now. That's all we wanted – him!

WHITAKER (*putting headphones on the table*): Why don't you keep quiet, Bamforth man! I got something on the set!

BAMFORTH: 'Course you did, my old flower of the East. What was it, Sammy Son? Henry Hall? Tune it up a bit – let's all have a listen. Bit of music always makes a change.

WHITAKER: I told you – I got something coming through.

MACLEISH: You think it was the camp?

BAMFORTH: We're fifteen miles from base. He's not Marconi. This boy couldn't get the Home Service in the sitting-room.

WHITAKER: I don't know what it was. I got something.

BAMFORTH: Fifteen miles from base! A doolally battery and ten-thumbed Whitaker i/c! What you want? A screaming miracle?

SMITH: Try them again, Sammy. Have another go.

MACLEISH: Try it on transmit.

EVANS: Tell them I'm coming home tomorrow night, boyo. Ask them in the cookhouse what's for supper. What's to-morrow? Friday? It's fish and chips!

SMITH: Do you think of anything except your stomach?

BAMFORTH: He's a walking belly.

    WHITAKER *sits down and replaces headphones. He picks up the microphone and adjusts the set.* BAMFORTH *and* EVANS *approach table.*

WHITAKER: Blue Patrol . . . Blue Patrol calling Red Leader . . . Blue Patrol calling Red Leader . . . Are you receiving me? . . . Are you receiving me? . . . Blue Patrol calling Red Leader . . . Are you receiving me? . . . Are you receiving me? . . . Over. (WHITAKER *flicks switch to 'receive'. There is a pause during which we hear some interference – but nothing else.* WHITAKER *flicks back to 'transmit'.*) Blue Patrol calling Red Leader . . . Are you receiving me? . . . Are you receiving me? . . . Over. (WHITAKER *again flicks to 'receive'. More interference.* WHITAKER *turns down the set and removes the headphones.*) It's dis. I think the battery's gone again.

BAMFORTH: So what's the use.

WHITAKER: I got something through, I tell you!

BAMFORTH: That's your story, boy. You stick to it.

EVANS: Perhaps you imagined it, Sammy boy.

WHITAKER: I had something coming through!

BAMFORTH: Don't give us that. Got through! You couldn't get through a hot dinner, my old son.

MACLEISH: Why don't you wrap up, Bamforth.

BAMFORTH: Eight-double seven Private Bamforth to you, Corporal MacLeish. You want to come the regimental, boy, we'll have it proper.

SMITH: That will be the day, Bamforth. When you can work it regimental. The biggest shower since the flood, that's you. Fred Karno's not in it. When you start giving us the heels together I'll be commanding the Camel Corps.

BAMFORTH: Get your bucket and spade, Smudger, and I'll lay it on. This boy can work it any way at all. If I go creeping after tapes I'll get them.

EVANS: Corporal Bamforth. N.C.O. i/c latrines. It's you who'll want the bucket, Bammo.

BAMFORTH: That's all you know, you Welsh rabbit. You'd be the first to suffer. I'll have you running round the depot like a blue-house fly. Report to my tent at 1600 hours. Extra duties. Gas cape and running shoes.

EVANS: And can I have a week-end pass?

BAMFORTH: You what! What do you think you're on? Your father's yacht?

SMITH: You get some kip, Taff. Dream of home. It's the nearest you'll get to Welsh Wales.

   BAMFORTH *crosses to form, picks up his pack, punches it into a pillow and lies down.* WHITAKER, *who has been attempting to tune set, puts on headphones and switches to 'transmit'.*

WHITAKER: Blue Patrol calling Red Leader . . . Blue Patrol calling Red Leader . . . Are you receiving me . . . Are you receiving me . . . Come in Red Leader . . . Over.

   WHITAKER *switches to 'receive' and again attempts to tune in set.* EVANS *opens his pack and takes out a crumpled magazine.* BAMFORTH *glances across at* EVANS.

BAMFORTH: What you got there, Taff?

EVANS: A book.

BAMFORTH: Two's up.

EVANS: I'll let you have it when I've finished.

BAMFORTH (*sitting up*): What is it? Sling it across.

EVANS (*crosses and sits on form*): My mother saves me them. (*He hands the magazine to* BAMFORTH.)

BAMFORTH: And you've been carting this around for days!

EVANS: Why not?

BAMFORTH: Here, Smudge! Seen this?

SMITH: What's that?

BAMFORTH: Taff's library.

SMITH: Yeh?

BAMFORTH: 'Ladies' Companion and Home.'

SMITH: Get on!

EVANS: My mother sends it to me every week. I'm following the serial. What's wrong with that?

BAMFORTH: And you've been humping this since we left camp? Well, flipping stroll on! That's all. Stroll on.

EVANS: Why not? I've told you. I'm following the serial.

SMITH: Any good, Taff?

EVANS: Yes. It's all right. It's interesting. There's this bloke, see. In the army. Second Looey. He's knocking about with this girl who's a sort of nurse in a Military Hospital. Only before they have time to get to know each other proper, he gets posted overseas.

MACLEISH: Very exciting.

BAMFORTH: I'm crying my eyes out!

SMITH: So what happens then, Taff?

EVANS: Thing is, see, she doesn't know anything about it.

BAMFORTH: He should have taught her.

EVANS: I mean about this overseas posting. He's supposed to meet this bint one night round the back of the Nurses' Quarters.

BAMFORTH: The dirty old man!

EVANS: Who's telling this story, Bammo? Me or you?

SMITH: Get on with it, Taff.

EVANS: I'm just coming to the interesting bit if you'll give me a chance.

BAMFORTH: Come on then. Give. Let's have it. I can hardly wait to hear how Roger gets on.

EVANS: That's just it. He doesn't.

BAMFORTH: I knew there'd be a catch in it.

EVANS: He never turns up, see. Been posted. Special Mission. Got to blow up an airfield in North Africa.

SMITH: What? On his tod?

EVANS: Last one I had he'd been captured by a tribe of marauding bedouins. Savage heathens.

SMITH: Get away!

EVANS: And it finished up the last time with them tying him, hand and foot, and hanging him upside down above a blazing fire. In a sort of oasis. There was him, toasting away if you like, with the sweat dripping down off the end of his nose. And these white-robed bedouins is dancing round, waving carbines, singing heathen songs and not a care in the world. That was how it finished up in the last instalment.

SMITH: So what happens this week?

EVANS: That's just it. I can't make head or tail of it. This week starts off with him and this here nursing bint having an honeymoon in Brighton. Posh hotel, made up to captain, fourteen days' leave, smashing girl and the weather's glorious. Doesn't make sense to me. I think perhaps the old lady slipped up and sent me the wrong one first.

BAMFORTH: She slipped up all right. When she had you. Marauding bedouins! You'll lap up any old muck.

SMITH: After you with it, anyway, Taff.

BAMFORTH: You wait your turn. I'm two's up. (*He flicks through the pages of the magazine.*) Here – this is the bit I like. 'Margaret Denning Replies.' All these bints writing up 'cause someone's left them in the lurch.

SMITH: Read us one out, Bammo.

BAMFORTH: Here's a right one. Get this. 'Dear Margaret Denning, I have been walking out for six months with a corporal in the Army who's a very nice boy.' Well, there's a lie for a kick-off.

EVANS: What's she want to know?

BAMFORTH: 'I like him very much and we plan to marry when the war is over. Lately, however, he has been making certain suggestions which I know are wrong.'

EVANS: Certain suggestions!

BAMFORTH: 'He says I ought to agree if I love him. What shall I do? Ought I to fall in with his wishes or should I stand by my principles and risk losing him? I have always wanted a white wedding. Yours, Gwynneth Rees, Aberystwyth.' It's another Taffy!

SMITH: So what's she tell her?

BAMFORTH: 'Dear Miss Taffy, I am sorry to hear that you have had the misfortune to fall in love with a corporal. The next time he starts making improper suggestions you should belt him one and marry a private.'

EVANS: It doesn't say that, does it?

BAMFORTH (*rises and slings the magazine at* EVANS): What do you think, you ignorant burk?

EVANS: Oh, I don't know . . . What do you reckon she ought to do, Smudge?

SMITH: Same as Bammo says.

EVANS: I don't know, really. I suppose you've got to wait until you're married, proper. I mean, it spoils it otherwise, they say. But if this bloke she's going out with is in the army, perhaps he's up for overseas posting himself. I mean, things is different when there is a war. You never know, do you? He might get pushed off overseas for years, perhaps. Then where would he be?

BAMFORTH: Same as you. Up the creek without a paddle.

EVANS: That's what I'm getting at.

BAMFORTH: Wrap up, boy! Look. Don't be a creamer all your life. Have a day off. You've got a bint yourself, have you? Back home?

EVANS: I've got a girl friend. Well, of course I have. You know as well as I do. You've seen her picture.

BAMFORTH: So when you see her last?

EVANS: Embarkation leave, of course. Over a year ago. Eighteen months about.

BAMFORTH: Eighteen months! Stroll on! For all you know she could be weaning one by now. You know what Blighty is these days, do you? It's a carve up, son. A rotten carve up. Overrun with home postings wallahs, sitting back easy, sorting out the judies from Land's End to how's your father. They've got it all laid on, son. We're the mugs in this game. It's a den of vice, is Blighty. Unoriginal sin. Poles and Yanks and cartloads of glorious allies all colours of the rainbow. Even the nippers look like liquorice all-sorts. They're lapping it up, Taff. You think the bints are sitting knitting?

EVANS: Mine's all right, boy. Don't you worry about that.

BAMFORTH: You mean you hope she is. You're a bloody optimist. She's probably up the mountains right this minute with a great big Yank.

EVANS: Go on, man! She's not like that.

BAMFORTH: They're all like that. So why should yours be any different?

EVANS: Well, if anything was wrong I'd hear about it.

BAMFORTH: Famous last words. What gives you that idea?

EVANS: Her mother's my auntie.

BAMFORTH: You can't marry her then! It's disgusting!

EVANS: Not my real auntie. She lives next door but one to us at home. I only call her my auntie. They've been friends, see, her mother and my mother for ever such a long time. My father's brother married her cousin, that's all. I've called her my auntie since I was a little lad.

BAMFORTH: You make it sound like rabbits.

EVANS: All the same, if anything was wrong with her, my mother would write and let me know.

BAMFORTH: You hope.

EVANS: Well, of course she would!

BAMFORTH: Look, son. Do yourself a favour, eh? Don't give me all that bull. There's only one way to keep them faithful. And that's like Smudger. Marry them sharpish and leave them with a couple of snappers running round the drum. Keep them occupied. With three or four nippers howling out for grub they don't have time to think. Right, Smudge?

SMITH: That's about it.

MACLEISH: I fail to see, Bamforth, what experience you've had on the subject.

BAMFORTH: Get lost, you Scotch haggis.

EVANS: How many you got, Smudge?

SMITH: Two.

EVANS: Boys?

SMITH: One of each.

EVANS: Boy and a girl. Must be smashing.

SMITH: What? Kids?

EVANS: Not only that. You know. Having home, like. You know, something to go back to – afterwards. Home of your own, I mean. Wife and family and home and that. Got a house of your own yet, have you?

SMITH: Bit of a one. Council. Up on the new estate.

EVANS: Go on!

SMITH: It's all right. Bit of a garden, not much, but it's all right. Better than nothing.

EVANS: Did you do any gardening, Smudge, before you came in the army?

SMITH: Not a lot. Few veg round the back – cabbages and that, brussels, couple of rows of peas, one or two blooms. Not a lot. You know – the usual.

EVANS: I know what you mean.

SMITH: Always left the front. Made a sort of a bit of a lawn of it. Sit out on Sundays on it after dinner. Me and the Missis. Saturday afternoons sometimes – when there was football on the wireless. Just big enough to sit on – two of you. Nice bit of grass. At least, it was. I suppose the kids have racked it up.

EVANS: You don't know. Perhaps the missis has been looking after it.

SMITH: Perhaps.

EVANS: Must be worse for you, I suppose. Being stuck out here. Not like the rest of us. Having a family to think about, I mean.

BAMFORTH: Well, don't let that get you down, Taff. By the time you get out of this lot your Cardiff bint'll be miles away with her Yank.

SMITH: That'd give the neighbours something to think about, Taff.

EVANS: I'd give her something to think about if she did.

BAMFORTH: Don't be like that, Taffy. Allies is allies, my old son. No good having allies if you're not willing to share what little bit you've got.

EVANS: They wouldn't be no allies of mine, then.

BAMFORTH: You're not democratic, that's your trouble.

EVANS (rises and throws magazine at BAMFORTH): I'll be after you, Bammo, if you don't give it a rest!

BAMFORTH: You and who else?

EVANS (crossing and playfully sparring up to BAMFORTH): Just me, boy. You're just my size.

BAMFORTH: Come on then, you Welsh Taff! Stick me one on!

EVANS: All right! You asked for it!

EVANS closes in on BAMFORTH and throws a punch. BAM-FORTH grabs Evans's hand and twists it up and round his *back.* BAMFORTH *flings* EVANS *to the floor, grabs a foot and twists it from the ankle.*

EVANS: Go steady, man! You'll break my leg!

BAMFORTH: You're an ignorant Welsh Taff! What are you? An ignorant Welsh Taff!

EVANS: Get off my leg, you rotten fool!

BAMFORTH: Say you're an ignorant Welsh Taff! Say you're an ignorant Welsh Taff!

EVANS: You'll break my leg!

WHITAKER (*adjusting radio controls*): Something coming through again!

BAMFORTH (*to* EVANS): Tell them! Come on, tell them what you are!

EVANS: Will you let go, man!

BAMFORTH: Tell them what you are.

EVANS: I'm an ignorant Welsh Taff . . . I'm an ignorant Welsh Taff!

MACLEISH: Bamforth! Evans! Knock it off, the pair of you!

BAMFORTH (*disengaging himself from* EVANS): So what's the matter now?

EVANS (*climbs to his feet*): You want to go easy, Bammo boy. You damn near crippled me.

BAMFORTH *and* EVANS *move across to where* WHITAKER *is seated. The radio operator is again attempting to contact base.*

WHITAKER (*flicking transmitter switch*): Blue Patrol . . . Blue Patrol calling Red Leader . . . Are you receiving me? . . . Are you receiving me? . . . Over . . . (WHITAKER *flicks to 'receive' and adjusts controls. He fades up the volume and we hear the crackle of interference on the set. For a moment there is also the sound of distorted speech on the radio – though the distortion and interference are too strong to make the voice distinguishable.*) It's there again!

EVANS: He's right, Bammo! I heard it myself.

BAMFORTH: Ah, so what.

EVANS: I heard voices, Bammo!

BAMFORTH: So what does that make you? Joan of Arc? What if you did? Could have been from any of the mobs up the jungle.

EVANS: Could have been base, boyo.

WHITAKER *takes off the headphones.*

MACLEISH: Could you make out what it was, Whitaker?

WHITAKER (*shakes his head*): Too much interference. (*He switches the set off.*) I'd better leave it. No sense in wasting the battery. I'll leave it now till Mitch gets back.

BAMFORTH (*crosses to form, picks up his pack and takes out a food pack*): You do that, son. You tell old mother Mitchem all about it. What a good boy you've been. Please, Sergeant, I've been working ever so hard. Please, Sergeant, I've been fiddling about with my little wireless all the time that you were out. Please, Sergeant, can I have a stripe? You make me sick. (*He tears open the food pack.*) Stroll on! Look here. Bungy. Bloody cheese again. I'll swing for that ration corporal one of these days.

EVANS: What do you reckon it was, Smudge?

SMITH: What's that?

EVANS: On the set. You think it might have been camp?

SMITH: Don't ask me. Whitaker's the boy to ask.

WHITAKER: Must have been. It's only fifteen miles to base. The nearest mob to us are nearly thirty miles up country.

EVANS: What the hell are we supposed to be doing anyway? Stuck here in the middle?

SMITH: Playing at soldiers. What they call a routine patrol, Taff. Keeping out of mischief. Out of the N.A.A.F.I. bar. It keeps you under control. Keeps the Colonel happy. It's good for morale.

EVANS: It's no good for my rotten feet. These boots, I think. The rubber soles that draw them.

BAMFORTH: It's a crumb patrol. It's just about the crummiest detail in the Far East is this, and no messing. Two days humping kit and two days back. Routine Patrol!

You can stick this for a game of soldiers. Talk about the
P.B.I. If every there was an all-time crumb patrol, we're on
it. (*He glances round at* WHITAKER, *who has taken a needle,
ball of wool and a pair of socks from his pack and is busily engaged
in darning.*) What the hell are you supposed to be doing?
(WHITAKER, *bent over his task, does not look up.*) You!

WHITAKER (*looks up*): What's up?

BAMFORTH: What are you on like?

WHITAKER: My socks.

BAMFORTH: What for?

WHITAKER: Kit inspection Saturday morning.

BAMFORTH: Well, that just about beats the lot, does that!
Now I've seen everything. Rotten stroll on! The third
day's hump we're on – three days out and bright boy's
sweating on a kit inspection! What with him and his
'Ladies' Companion' and you and your knitting! You'll
still be at it when the Japs get here.

MACLEISH: And where will you be, Bamforth?

BAMFORTH: Me?

MACLEISH: When the Japs arrive?

BAMFORTH: Not here, that's certain. I wasn't meant to be
a hero.

MACLEISH: I gathered that.

BAMFORTH: I'll tell you where I'll be, boy. Scarpering. Using
my loaf. On the trot. I've got it all worked out. The lot.
Tin of Cherry Blossom Dark Tan from head to foot. Couple
of banana leaves round my old whatsits. Straight through
Kew Gardens outside and head for the water. Like one of
the locals.

EVANS: You reckon you could make it, Bammo?

BAMFORTH: What! If the yellow hordes were waving
bayonets at me I'd be off like a whippet. You'll not see my
tail for dust. There's more wog rowing boats up the coast
than enough. Nip off in one of them and straight to sea.

SMITH: On your own?

BAMFORTH: Tod or nothing. When the time comes, Smudge, it's going to be every man for himself.

EVANS: Go on, man. Where could you make for?

BAMFORTH: What's it matter? Anywhere but here. Desert Island. One that's loaded with bags of native bints wearing grass frocks. Settle down and turn native. Anything's better than ending up with Tojo's boys.

EVANS: You'd never do it.

BAMFORTH: That's all you know. Come down the beach and wave me off. If you've got time to wave with all them little Nippos on your trail. I'll be in the boat, Jack. Lying back and getting sunburnt with a basket of coconuts. (*'Cod'* American.) And so we say farewell to this lush, green and prosperous country of Malaya. As the sun sets in the west our tiny boat bobs peacefully towards the horizon. We take one last glimpse at the beautiful tropical coastline and can see, in the distance, our old comrade in arms and hopeless radio operator, Private Whitaker, making peace with the invading army of the Rising Sun – and the invading army of the Rising Sun is carving pieces out of Private Whitaker.

WHITAKER (*rising*): Pack it in, Bamforth.

BAMFORTH: What's the matter, Whitto? Getting windy?

WHITAKER: Just pack it in, that's all.

BAMFORTH: Get knotted.

MACLEISH: I haven't seen anybody handing medals to you yet, Bamforth.

BAMFORTH: No, my old haggis basher. And you're not likely to. I've told you – I don't go a bundle on this death or glory stuff.

MACLEISH: So why not keep your trap shut.

BAMFORTH: Democracy, Mac. Free Speech. Votes for women and eight-double-seven Private Bamforth for Prime Minister.

SMITH: Show us your Red Flag, Bammo.

BAMFORTH: It's what we're fighting for. Loose living and six months' holiday a year. The General told me that himself. 'Bamforth,' he says to me, taking me round the back of the lav at Catterick. 'Bammo, my old son, the British Army's in a desperate position. The yellow peril's about to descend upon us, the gatling's jammed, the Colonel's dead and the cook corporal's stuffed the regimental mascot in the oven. On top of all that, and as if we hadn't got enough to worry about, we've got two thousand Jocks up the jungle suffering from screaming ab-dabs.and going mad for women, beer and haggis. We're posting you out there, Bammo,' he says, 'to relieve the situation.' So before I had time to relieve myself, here I was.

MACLEISH: And what have you got against the Jocks?

BAMFORTH: Stroll on! He's off again! It's a joke, you thick-skulled nit!

MACLEISH: And I'll not stand for any of your insubordinations.

BAMFORTH: Come on, boy! Come it on! Pull the tape on me again. That's all I want. I'll blanco your belt for you for twopence.

MACLEISH: When you're on duty, Bamforth, you'll take orders like the rest.

BAMFORTH: Get the ink dry in your pay-book first. You've not had the tape a month.

MACLEISH: If I'm in charge here, that's all that matters, as far as you're concerned. It makes no difference to you if I've had the tape five minutes or five years. You'll jump to it, boy, when I'm calling out the time. You'll just do as you're told, or you're for the high jump. (BAMFORTH *swears under his breath and turns away.*) Bamforth! Bamforth, I'm talking to you!

BAMFORTH (*swings round*): Private Bamforth! I've got a rank myself, acting unpaid unwanted Lance Corporal Macleish!

MACLEISH: Evans!

EVANS: Corp?

MACLEISH: Come here. (*As* EVANS *crosses towards the window* MACLEISH *tosses him the rifle.*) Here. You're on guard. Take over from me.

EVANS: Corp.

MACLEISH (*crosses down to face* BAMFORTH): I'm not giving you any second warnings, Bamforth. When you speak to me you'll watch your mouth. I mean that, Bamforth, just watch out – or as sure as I'm standing here, I'll have you.

BAMFORTH: Try taking off your tape and saying that, you Scotch get.

MACLEISH: I've already told you, this has got nothing to do with the tape. I'm not warning you for C.O.'s orders, boy. I'm not interested in having you on the C.O.'s veranda with your cap and belt off. One word to me and I'll put your teeth down your throat. I mean that.

BAMFORTH: What with?

MACLEISH (*raising his fists*): These. Just these.

BAMFORTH (*unfastening his jacket*): If you want to play it the hard way, Jock . . .

MACLEISH: I want to play it any way that suits me. And right now it suits me to sort you out.

SMITH (*crossing from window*): Wrap it up, Jock.

MACLEISH: You keep out of this, Smudge. This has got nothing to do with you – it's personal between Bamforth and myself – it's got nothing to do with you.

SMITH: Like hell it hasn't. You're like a couple of kids.

MACLEISH: I said, keep out of it!

SMITH: Grow up! For God's sake grow up, the pair of you! What do you think you're on?

BAMFORTH: I'm waiting for you, Jock.

SMITH: So go on, Mac. You take a poke at him and where's it get you? You lose your tape, you're in the nick.

MACLEISH: The tape means nothing to me.

SMITH: So all right! You get six months in the nick.

BAMFORTH: What are you waiting for? You're pretty big with the mouth, Jock; let's see you follow it up.

MACLEISH (*raising his fists and moving in on* BAMFORTH): You asked for it . . .

SMITH (*restraining* MACLEISH): You dim Scotch crone! It's what he wants! He's dying for you to put him one on. Use your loaf! Sling in your tape and stick him one on then – if it's going to make you feel any better. Do it then. You put a finger on him now he'll come King's Regs on you so fast your feet won't touch the ground.

MACLEISH (*shrugging* SMITH *away*): I'll sort him so he never comes King's Regs again. On me or anybody else!

EVANS has turned away from the window and all interest is centred on MACLEISH *and* BAMFORTH *as the door opens and* MITCHEM *and* JOHNSTONE *enter.*

MITCHEM: So what's all this in aid of?

JOHNSTONE: Do your jacket up, Bamforth!

BAMFORTH: Must have come undone.

JOHNSTONE: And get your heels together when you speak to me, lad!

BAMFORTH (*coming slowly to attention*): Corporal.

There is an apprehensive pause as MITCHEM *crosses slowly into the centre of the room.*

MITCHEM: On your feet! (WHITAKER *rises.*) Get fell in, the lot of you! Move yourselves! (*The members of the patrol, with the exception of* JOHNSTONE, *fall in in single rank.*) Ted, stand by the door.

JOHNSTONE (*half closes the door and stands on guard*): Check.

MITCHEM (*he walks slowly along the line of men and turns, flicking open an unbuttoned breast pocket on* EVANS'S *jacket as he walks back.* EVANS *steps one pace out of the ranks, fastens the button and moves back into line.* MITCHEM *looks along the line of men. There is a long pause before he speaks.*): Shower! Useless shower! That's all you are. The lot of you. I could have been a regiment of ruddy Nips and I walked through that door. I walked straight in! . . . Squad – shun! Stand at ease. Squad – shun! Stand at ease. Corporal Macleish!

MACLEISH (*steps one pace forward smartly*): Sarnt!

MITCHEM: I left you in charge.

MACLEISH: Sarnt!

MITCHEM: So what happened?

MACLEISH: I . . . I had occasion to reprimand . . . I'm sorry, Sergeant. I forgot myself for the moment.

MITCHEM (*pause*): So you're sorry. You forgot yourself. I leave you in charge of the section for ten minutes and the whole organization goes to pot. Ten minutes, Corporal, and you're running a monkey house! (*Pause.* MITCHEM *walks along the line and back.*) You had occasion to reprimand who?

MACLEISH: I . . . I forget now, Sergeant. It was one of the men.

MITCHEM: I didn't think it was a chimpanzee. Who was it?

MACLEISH: It was something that happened in the heat of the moment. I forget now.

MITCHEM: Then you'd better remember. Smartish. Corporal Macleish, who was the man?

MACLEISH: If it's all the same to you, Sergeant, I'd prefer not to say.

MITCHEM: For your information, Macleish, it's not the same to me. Just what do you think this is? Just what? All girls together and no telling tales? You think I'm running a Sunday School outing? 'Please, Miss, it was Jimmie Smith who sat on the tomato sandwiches but I promised not to tell.' (EVANS *laughs.*) Shut up!

MACLEISH: It was a personal matter I'd prefer to handle in my own way.

MITCHEM: Then let me put you straight, Corporal. Right now. Before it's too late. You haven't got no personal matters. Not while you're out with me. While you were settling it in your own way – sorting out your personal matters – you could have had seven men, including yourself, with their tripes on the floor. Remember that. Seven.

Including me. And as far as I'm concerned, what happens to me's important. (*Addressing the patrol.*) To look at some of you the army's not gained all that much by his incompetence. But, all the same, I brought you out and I intend to take you back. The lot of you. I'll not stand any more from any one of you who makes it awkward for the rest. I want the man who started all this argument to stand out now . . . Come on, come on! (*There is a pause.*) All right. Fair enough. Have it how you want. You'll all be on fatigues when we get back to camp.

MACLEISH: You can't punish all the section.

MITCHEM: I can do just what I like, Corporal. I can have your guts for garters if I want.

MACLEISH: It's against all army regulations.

   BAMFORTH *takes one pace forward.*

MITCHEM (*crossing to face* BAMFORTH): Hello! What's this? I was wrong. It was a chimpanzee. As if I hadn't guessed. Private Bamforth, eight-double-seven.

BAMFORTH: Sarnt!

MITCHEM: Coming it on again. Coming it on. It's about time you and me had a few words.

BAMFORTH: Sarnt?

MITCHEM: Now get this, Bamforth. Get it straight. Get it in your head. Since you've been posted out to join this mob it's crossed my mind, a time or two, that you don't like the army.

BAMFORTH: Sarnt.

MITCHEM: It's a mutual feeling, Bamforth. The army's not in love with you. If I had you in my lot in Blighty, lad, you wouldn't last a week. I've met your kind before. I've seen men who'd make a breakfast out of muck like you go in the nick and do their time and come back so that butter wouldn't melt between their crutch. Don't try and come the hard-case stuff with me, son. It doesn't work. I'm up to all them tricks myself. O.K.

BAMFORTH: Sarnt.

MITCHEM: I've watched you, lad. I've had my eye on you. Ever since you first turned up. I've seen you try and come it on with every junior N.C.O. that's been made up. The barrack-room lawyer. The hard case. You can quote King's Regs from now until the middle of next week. Up to every dodge and skive that's in the book. There's just one thing. It doesn't work with me, 'cause I don't work according to the book. You don't know anything, Bamforth. You don't know anything at all. But if you want to try and come it on with me I'll tell you, here and now, that I can be a bastard. I can be the biggest bastard of them all. And just remember this: I've got three stripes start on you. You're a non-runner, son, I start favourite halfway down the course before the off. You haven't got a chance. So now just go ahead and play it how you want. I'm easy. (*Pause.*) Now get back into line the pair of you. Move! (MACLEISH *and* BAMFORTH *step back into the rank.* MITCHEM *crosses to speak to* BAMFORTH.) And if you take my tip you'll stay in line. (MITCHEM *steps back to address the patrol.*) Stand at ease! . . . Easy . . . (*The men relax.*) Now, pay attention – all of you. We've had a sortie round, Corporal Johnstone and myself; I'll try and put you in the picture now before we set off back. The main track is about sixty yards from here through the trees. The way we came – and that's the way we're going back. Round the back of here the undergrowth's so thick it would take a month of Sundays to hack half a mile. There's only one way out and that's where we came in. It's over fifteen miles from here to camp and we're moving off in fifteen minutes' time. We march at five-yard intervals – I don't want any of you closing up. Corporal Johnstone's breaking trail and I'll bring up the rear. There'll be no talking. I've said there'll be a five-yard interval between each man. You'll keep it that way. What goes for closing up goes twice as much for dropping back – I don't want any of you falling out. I've told you once it's fifteen miles, or thereabouts, to base. Due south. The other way – north – and twenty miles as near as we can estimate, the line's been built to keep the Nips at bay. All positions have been consolidated. Which means that all the mobs from round these parts have moved up to the front – or most of them – a few have been withdrawn. There's not a living soul, apart from local wogs, if any, for miles from here. If any one of you gets lost he's on his own. I don't advise it. So you keep it five yards – dead. Anybody any questions?

MACLEISH: Sergeant?

MITCHEM: Yeh?

MACLEISH: Have you any idea which of the mobs have moved up country?

MITCHEM: Only what I heard when we left camp. And they were rumours in the mess. Just about the lot, they reckon. The Fusiliers, two regiments of Jocks and some Artillery. You studying Military History?

MACLEISH: No. I've got . . . It's my brother. He's with the Highland boys.

MITCHEM: I see.

MACLEISH: He's my young brother. We've applied to get his transfer to our mob. It's not come through yet. You've heard they've moved them up already?

MITCHEM: It was just a rumour in the mess . . . Anybody else got any ticks? (*There is a negative murmur from the men.*) That makes a change. Right then. Fifteen minutes and we push off back. Who did first stag?

MACLEISH: Smith and myself, Sergeant.

MITCHEM: You two had better have a break. Bamforth, Evans!

BAMFORTH:⎫ Sarge?
EVANS: ⎭

MITCHEM: You're both on guard. All right. The rest of you fall out.

BAMFORTH *and* EVANS *pick up their rifles and cross to windows.* MACLEISH *and* SMITH *cross to form and sit down.* JOHNSTONE *closes door and crosses into room as the two reliefs reach the windows.*

MITCHEM: Whitaker!

WHITAKER: Sergeant?

MITCHEM: Any joy on the set?

WHITAKER: I got something through about five minutes ago, Sarge. I don't know what it was, though. Too faint to pick it up.

JOHNSTONE (*crossing to join* MITCHEM *and* WHITAKER): You got through to base, did you say, Whitaker?

WHITAKER: No, Corp. I got something through, though. I was telling the Sergeant. I picked up something but I don't know what it was.

JOHNSTONE: How much a week do they pay you for this, lad?

MITCHEM: It's not his fault. The battery's dis. O.K., Sammy. Have another go. Better give it one more try.

WHITAKER (*sitting down at set*): Right, Sergeant. (*He tunes in the set behind following dialogue.*)

JOHNSTONE: What you reckon, Mitch?

MITCHEM: What's that?

JOHNSTONE: What he got?

MITCHEM: Dunno . . . Suppose it must have been the camp. No one else in this area pushing out signals. With a wonky set he couldn't pick up any of the front-line mobs from here. They're out of range. So it figures that it must have been the camp.

JOHNSTONE: I'd like to put the boot in on the burk who dished us out with a u/s batt. S.O.B., that's all they are, the H.Q. men.

MITCHEM: We'll sort that out when we get back.

JOHNSTONE: I'd like to ram his pig-muck battery down his throat, that's all. Who was on duty in the battery shop?

MITCHEM: It's no good flapping over that. We'll let him have another go and if nothing comes up we'll pack it in. Push off back. We've got a negative report. It doesn't make a lot of difference.

JOHNSTONE: It could have been something else. It could have been important.

MITCHEM: It isn't. So we can sort it out when we get back.

JOHNSTONE and MITCHEM *turn and listen as* WHITAKER *attempts to make contact.*

WHITAKER: Blue Patrol to Red Leader . . . Blue Patrol calling Red Leader . . . Are you receiving me? . . . are you receiving me? . . . Come in, Red Leader, come in Red Leader . . . Over.

WHITAKER *flicks to 'receive' and tunes in. Sound of interference held behind.* JOHNSTONE *and* MITCHEM *listen for a moment and then turn away.*

JOHNSTONE: Damn duff equipment! The whole damn issue's duff.

MITCHEM (*takes out a packet of cigarettes and offers one to* JOHN-STONE): Fag?

JOHNSTONE (*taking the cigarette*): Ta. (*He takes a box of matches from his box, strikes one, offers a light to* MITCHEM, *then lights his own.*)

MITCHEM (*inhales deeply then exhales*): Thanks.

JOHNSTONE: Time do you reckon we'll get back?

MITCHEM: Tomorrow? 'Bout 1800 hours if we keep it up. Roll on. Roll on, let's get some kip.

JOHNSTONE: If you get the chance. Kit inspection Saturday morning. What's the betting we end up on the square after all? C.O.'s parade.

MITCHEM: Not this boy. I'm going to grab a week-end off, and chuff the expense.

WHITAKER (*pushes the headphones on to the back of his head and turns in his chair*): Sarge!

MITCHEM (*turns*): Yeh?

WHITAKER: Coming through again!

MITCHEM and JOHNSTONE cross to the table and listen intently to the set. WHITAKER replaces headphones and tunes in. MACLEISH and SMITH, who have been talking together on the form, sit up and listen. There is an air of expectancy amongst the patrol. As WHITAKER fiddles with the controls the interference increases and dies away. A faint murmur of speech can be heard from the set.

WHITAKER: There it is!

MITCHEM: Come on, lad! Let's be having it.

EVANS: Ask the C.O. if he loves me as much as always, Whitto boy!

BAMFORTH: Nobody loves you, you horrible Taff!

JOHNSTONE: Shut up! Pack the talking in!

WHITAKER: I've got it now!

The radio bursts into life. The voice of a Japanese radio operator comes through the set clearly. WHITAKER turns and looks in bewilderment at MITCHEM. These two are the first to realize the implications. There is a slight pause, stemming from surprise, then the patrol reacts with forced humour.

BAMFORTH: You've got it, Whitto son, all right. You've got the ruddy Japs.

EVANS: If that's the camp they're having rice for tea and my name's Tojo.

BAMFORTH: Bring on the geisha girls!

MACLEISH: A right ruddy radio operator you've turned out to be, Whitaker. You don't know who's side you're on.

MITCHEM (*leans across and switches off the set*): Pack the talking in, the lot of you! Right, Whitaker. (WHITAKER, *who is staring in horror at the set, makes no reply.*) Whitaker, I'm talking to you, lad! (WHITAKER *looks up for the first time.*) How strong's the battery? . . . Come on, come on!

WHITAKER: It's almost gone. The battery's nearly dead.

MITCHEM: So what's your range at present? . . . Whitaker, your range?

WHITAKER (*pulling himself together slightly*): It must be under fifteen miles. I can't get through to camp. It could be ten. It might be less.

With the exception of EVANS *the patrol begins to comprehend.*

EVANS: Go on, Whitto boy! You're up the creek all over. The Japs are past Jalim Besar. It's twenty miles away at least.

SMITH: We're all up the creek.

BAMFORTH: Stroll on!

JOHNSTONE: Evans! Bamforth! You're supposed to be on guard! Get on your posts!

    EVANS *and* BAMFORTH, *who have turned away from the windows during the above dialogue, return to their positions.*

WHITAKER: It was as clear as a bell! They could be sitting right on top of us!

MACLEISH: Under fifteen miles away! So what's happened to the lads up country?

MITCHEM: Shut up.

MACLEISH: What's happened to the forward boys?

MITCHEM: Shut up.

MACLEISH: I've got my brother posted up out there!

MITCHEM: Shut up! Johnno, check the stens.

JOHNSTONE (*crossing to table where he checks* MITCHEM'S *sten and his own*): Right.

MITCHEM (*crossing to* MACLEISH): Now just shut up. Listen. All of you. Evans, Bamforth, don't turn round. I want your eyes out there. You got that, both of you? (BAMFORTH *and* EVANS *nod.*) Then ram a round apiece up your spouts. (BAMFORTH *and* EVANS *release the safety catches on their rifles, withdraw the bolts and slam them home.*) O.K. Now put your safety catches on. (BAMFORTH *and* EVANS *hesitate a moment and then comply.*) O.K. That's fine. That's all we need. No more than that. (*He crosses Centre Stage to address the patrol.*) Fred Karno's mob. That's what you are. Fred Karno's mob. There's half of you been shooting off your mouths for days on end on how you'd fix the Japs. To listen to you talk you'd win the ruddy war on bread and jam. You've heard one slimy Nippo on the set and now you're having second thoughts. You make me laugh, that's what you do to me – make me want to laugh. (JOHNSTONE *has now finished his examination of the stens.*) O.K., Johnno?

JOHNSTONE: Both O.K.

MITCHEM (*to the patrol*): You've heard one Nippo on the set. That might mean anything at all. It might mean that they've broken through, up country, and are pouring down. If that's a fact, then chuff your luck. That's all – just chuff your luck. They might be swarming out there now – like ants. And if they are and I'm with crumbs like you, I'm up the creek myself and that's a fact. (*The patrol murmurs uneasily.*) But all you know so far is that you've heard a Nippo griping on the set. And that could mean that somewhere in this festering heat one lousy bunch of Japs have wriggled in behind our lines – that could be half a dozen men. It could be less than that. It could be half a dozen joskins like yourselves. Six or seven – five or six – or even two or three poor helpless wet-nurse ginks who somewhere, close to here, are running round in circles, doing their nuts, because they've heard young Whitto pushing out a signal back to base. If that's the way things are with them, the bloke who's calling out the time for 'em has got my sympathy. I wish him luck. He's up to the short hairs in it like myself and so I wish him luck. (*The confidence of the men has been largely restored – one or two are even amused.*) I'll tell you what we're going to do. We're moving off. Right now. (*Murmur of relief from the men.*) We're going back. It's odds on that they're just a buckshee bunch of Harries like yourselves. All the same, we're not waiting to find out. The orders for the movement back still stand. Evans, Bamforth, you'll stay on guard until the others have got their gear on and are ready to move off back.

The men begin to struggle into their webbing equipment.

JOHNSTONE: Come on, then! Move yourselves! We've not got time to play about!

MITCHEM: Macleish and Smith! (MACLEISH *and* SMITH *pause in assembling their kit.*) Soon as you've got into your gear, relieve the two on guard and let them get theirs on. (MACLEISH *and* SMITH *nod and return to their task.*) Quick as you can.

JOHNSTONE (*picks up the stens and hands one to* MITCHEM): You want me to lead off back?

MITCHEM (*nods*): Crack the whip a bit. Set a steady pace. I want to try and do it in one stint.

JOHNSTONE: I'm with you.

BAMFORTH (*unnoticed by the others,* BAMFORTH *suddenly tenses himself and raises his rifle. He flicks off the safety catch and takes aim*): Sarge . . . Sarge!

MITCHEM (*sensing* BAMFORTH'S *urgency*): Hold it, all of you! (*The men are still and silent.*) What's up?

BAMFORTH: I thought I saw a movement down the track . . . It's there again!

MITCHEM (*to the patrol*): Get down! Get out of sight! (*Apart from the two men on guard and* MITCHEM, *the members of the patrol stoop below the level of the windows.*) How many of them? Can you see?

BAMFORTH (*lowers his rifle*): No. Out of sight again. Behind the trees. Heading this way.

MITCHEM, *his head down below window level, moves across the hut to join* BAMFORTH *at the window.* JOHNSTONE *moves across to join* EVANS.

MITCHEM: Which way they coming from?

BAMFORTH (*pointing*): Along the track. Down there. 'Bout fifty yards.

MITCHEM: Evans?

EVANS: Can't see a ruddy thing from here, Sarge. Not as far as that.

JOHNSTONE: There's a clump of blasted bushes in the way.

MITCHEM: Were they Japs?

BAMFORTH: Might have been anything. Only had a glimpse.

MITCHEM: Are you sure, Bamforth?

BAMFORTH: Meaning what?

MITCHEM: You saw anything at all, lad?

BAMFORTH: You think I'm going round the bend!

MITCHEM: All right. We'll take your word for it. If there is anyone down there they should come into sight again just by that bit of . . .

BAMFORTH (*nudges* MITCHEM *and points again*): A Jap!

MITCHEM: I've got him. On his own. (*Turns slightly from window.*) Now keep still, all of you. This one's on his tod. Could be a scout. He hasn't spotted this place up to press. Got him, Johnno?

JOHNSTONE: Can't see anything for this ruddy bush. Whereabouts?

MITCHEM: Just less than fifty yards. Straight ahead . . . Got him, have you?

JOHNSTONE: Not yet. What do you think he's on?

BAMFORTH: He's . . . He's looking round for something. In the grass. Looking for something . . Bending down.

JOHNSTONE: Think he's found the trail, Mitch? Up to here?

MITCHEM: Looks like that. Found something by the way he's carrying on.

   BAMFORTH *bursts into laughter.*

MITCHEM: Shut up!

BAMFORTH: Found the trail! He's found the trail all right! He's found a place to have a crafty smoke.

EVANS: He's what, Bammo?

BAMFORTH: Having a drag. He's lighting up a fag. Well, the crafty old Nip. The skiving get. Caught red-handed. Nip down and ask him for a puff, Taff.

MITCHEM: Of all the rotten luck. He would choose this place. We'll wait and see'f he pushes off . . . (BAMFORTH *slowly raises his rifle and takes careful aim.* MITCHEM *swings round and knocks the rifle out of aiming position.*) I said no noise!

BAMFORTH: I had him right between the cheeks! I couldn't miss! He's on his tod!

MITCHEM: What gives you that idea? Do you think they march off by the dozen for a sly swallow?

JOHNSTONE: What's happening?

BAMFORTH: He's up. He's standing up and nicking out the nub. He's going back. The way he came . . . Stopped . . . Turning round . . . He's coming back. He's found the track up here. He's coming up.

MITCHEM: Move it then, the rest of you. Let's have you over by the wall! And bring your gear.

MACLEISH, WHITAKER *and* SMITH *pick up their rifles and the kit and scurry across to the rear wall of the hut.*

MITCHEM (*peering round the window*): Bamforth, Evans, down on deck! (BAMFORTH *and* EVANS *drop below window level.*) And stay there all of you. There's just a chance he might not come inside. In case he does – Johnno . . . (MITCHEM *indicates the door.* JOHNSTONE *nods and sidles across to stand by the door.* MITCHEM *peers round window.*) If he should come in – you grab. Without a sound. I'll cover the outside in case. Still coming up . . . Close to the wall as you can. He might not see us yet.

WHITAKER (*notices the radio which is still standing on the table*): Sarge! The set!

MITCHEM: Oh God, lad! Get it! Quick! (WHITAKER *moves as if to cross to table, but changes his mind and hugs the wall in terror.* Get the set! (WHITAKER *is still afraid to move.* SMITH *is about to fetch the radio when we hear the sound of feet on the wooden veranda.*) Too late!

The members of the patrol squeeze up against the wall as MITCHEM *edges away from the window out of sight.* JOHNSTONE *tenses himself. The* JAPANESE SOLDIER *can be heard clattering on the veranda for several seconds before he appears at the Left Hand window. He peers into the room but fails to see the patrol and is just about to turn away when he notices the radio on the table. He stares at it for a short while and then moves out of sight as he crosses along the veranda towards the door. A further short pause,* JOHNSTONE *raises his hands in readiness. The door opens and the* JAPANESE SOLDIER *enters. As he steps into the room* JOHNSTONE *lunges forward and grabs the* JAPANESE, *putting an arm round his throat and his free hand over the soldier's mouth.* MITCHEM, *holding the sten at his hip, darts out of the door and covers the jungle from the veranda.* JOHNSTONE *and* THE PRISONER *struggle in the room.*

JOHNSTONE: Come on then, one of you! Get him! Quick! . . . Evans! Do for him! (EVANS *crosses and raises his rifle, releasing the safety catch.*) No, you burk! You want to do for me as well? Come on, lad! Use your bayonet! In his guts! You'll have to give it hump. (EVANS *unsheaths his bayonet and approaches the struggling figures.*) Sharp then, lad! Come on! Come on! You want it in between his ribs. (EVANS *raises the bayonet to stab* THE PRISONER, *who squirms in terror.*) Not that way, lad! You'll only bust a bone. Feel for it first, then ram it in. Now, come on, quick! (EVANS *places his bayonet point on the chest of* THE PRISONER, *who has now stopped struggling and is cringeing in the grip of* JOHN-STONE.) Come on! Come on! I can't hold on to him for ever! Will you ram it in!

EVANS (*steps back*): I . . . I can't do it, Corp.

JOHNSTONE: Stick it in! Don't stand there tossing up the odds! Just close your eyes and whoof it in!

EVANS: I can't! I can't! Corp, I can't.

JOHNSTONE: Macleish!

MACLEISH: Not me!

JOHNSTONE: Smith! Take the bayonet! Don't stand there gawping. Do the job!

SMITH: For God's sake do it, Taff. Put the poor bastard out of his misery.

EVANS (*proffering the bayonet to* SMITH): You!

BAMFORTH (*crossing and snatching the bayonet from* EVANS): Here. Give me hold. It's only the same as carving up a pig. Hold him still.

 BAMFORTH *raises the bayonet and is about to thrust it into the chest of the prisoner as* MITCHEM *enters, closing the door behind him.*

MITCHEM: Bamforth! Hold it!

BAMFORTH (*hesitates, then moves away*): I'm only doing what I'm told.

MITCHEM: Just hold it, that's all. I want this one alive. You'll have your chance before we've done. You can count on that. So pack in all this greyhound with a bunny lark. He's not the only one; you'll have your chance. How is he, Johnno? Is he going to do his nut?

JOHNSTONE: Scared stiff. He's going up the wall. I've had enough of him – he stinks of garlic and wog grub. He won't try anything – I wouldn't trust his mouth.

MITCHEM: Hold him for a sec. (MITCHEM *crosses close up to* THE PRISONER.) You speakee English? Understand? Compronney? Eh? Eh? You speakee English talk? Trust me to cop a raving lunatic. You! I want no noise, see? Understand? No noise! Quiet. (MITCHEM *points to his mouth and shakes his head.*) No speakee! Keep your trap shut, eh? Now get this, Tojo. Understand. You make so much as a mutter and I'll let Jack the Ripper have a go at you. (MITCHEM *indicates* BAMFORTH, *who is still holding the bayonet.* THE PRISONER *cringes in Johnstone's grip.*) O.K.? (MITCHEM *points again to his mouth and* THE PRISONER *nods vigorously.*) Good. One murmur, Jap, and Laughing Boy will slit your guts up to your ears. Universal talk. I think I'm getting through to him at last. Bamforth!

BAMFORTH (*crossing to* MITCHEM): Sarge?

MITCHEM: Put the carving knife away before he dies on us of fright.

BAMFORTH (*turns the bayonet over in his hand and makes a quick, playful gesture with the weapon towards the Prisoner's throat.* THE PRISONER *struggles again in Johnstone's arms*): Boo!

MITCHEM: Bamforth! Jack it in! I said put the cutlery away.

BAMFORTH: All right! (*He crosses and returns the bayonet to* EVANS *who replaces it in the sheath.* THE PRISONER *calms down.*) Thanks, Taff.

MITCHEM: Right, Johnno. He'll behave himself. He'll be a good lad. Put him down.

JOHNSTONE *pushes* THE PRISONER *away.* MITCHEM *gestures with the sten and the Prisoner's arms fly up above his head.* THE PRISONER *is a small, round, pathetic and almost comic character, armed to the teeth in a Gilbertian fashion: a revolver in a leather holster is slung round his chest and a string of hand grenades swings from his waist. A long two-edged bayonet hangs from his belt. He wears a drab, ill-fitting uniform, peaked cap and a white silk muffler is tied round his throat. As* THE PRISONER *stands alone and afraid in the centre of the hut the patrol cluster round to examine him.*

EVANS: He looks as if he's going to fight the war himself.

MACLEISH: He's not exactly what you'd call a handsome bloke.

MITCHEM: All right, get back. What do you want, Jock? A blonde? I'll fix it so it's Rita Hayworth walks in next. Move it! Back!

The members of the patrol cross over to the left as MITCHEM *ushers* THE PRISONER *towards the Right Hand wall.*

JOHNSTONE: Come on then! Move yourselves! He doesn't put the wind up you lot now? You're round him like a lot of lambs that's had their first taste of milk. Two minutes since you wouldn't touch him with a barge pole. None of you!

MITCHEM: Bamforth! Take the armoury away.

BAMFORTH (*crosses to* THE PRISONER, *who cringes away as he approaches*): Stand still, you nig! Unless you want the boot! (BAMFORTH *proceeds to remove the weapons from* THE PRISONER, *also checking him for any further arms.*)

JOHNSTONE: A right lot I've got landed with! Not one of you had the guts to give me a hand.

MACLEISH: You weren't in need of help. You cannot order men to put a bayonet in an unarmed prisoner.

JOHNSTONE: What do you think they dish you out with bayonets for? Just opening tins of soup?

MACLEISH: They're not to put in prisoners of war!

JOHNSTONE: You know what you can do with yours. You wouldn't know which end is which!

MACLEISH: If the need should arise I'll use a bayonet with the next. But I've no intention of using one on any man who can't defend himself.

JOHNSTONE: You burk!

MACLEISH: He was a prisoner of war!

JOHNSTONE: Prisoner my crutch!

MACLEISH: There's such a thing as the Geneva Convention!

JOHNSTONE: He's carting more cannon than the Woolwich Arsenal! If he'd have pulled the pin on one of them grenades we'd all of us been up the shoot! You think that he'd have second thoughts before he put the mockers on the lot of us?

BAMFORTH (*places the Prisoner's arms on the table*): That's about the lot.

MITCHEM: Which of you men's supposed to be on guard? The war's not won because you've copped a Nip!

EVANS: I was, Sarge.

MITCHEM: Get on your post and stay there, lad. Who else?

BAMFORTH: Me.

MITCHEM: I've got another job for you. Anybody else that's not done stag so far?

WHITAKER: I haven't been on guard yet, Sarge. I was on the set.

MITCHEM: Then get on now. Take Bamforth's number.

(EVANS *and* WHITAKER *pick up their rifles and cross to the windows.*) Bamforth!

BAMFORTH: Sarge?

MITCHEM (*offering his sten to* BAMFORTH): Here. Cop on for this. You're looking after Tojo here. I think he fancies you. If he tries to come it on he gets it through the head. No messing. He's on your charge. Look after him.

BAMFORTH (*shakes his head, refusing the sten*): Like he was my only chick. (BAMFORTH *picks up the Prisoner's bayonet from the table.*) I'll settle for this. (*He crosses towards* THE PRISONER.) Down, Shortarse. (*He motions* THE PRISONER *to sit on the form.*) Put your hands up on your head. (THE PRISONER *looks at* BAMFORTH *in bewilderment.*) I said, get your hands up on your head! Like this! See! Flingers on the blonce! All light? (BAMFORTH *demonstrates and* THE PRISONER *complies.* BAMFORTH *is delighted.*) Hey, Taff! See that, did you? He did it like I said! Flingers up on blonce. I only talk the lingo natural!

EVANS (*turning at window*): I always knew you were an Oriental creep at heart, man!

BAMFORTH: You've not seen nothing, yet – get this. (*To* THE PRISONER.) Allee lightee. Flingers up to touch the loof. Come on, come on! Touch the loof, you asiatic glet! (BAMFORTH *raises the bayonet and* THE PRISONER *cringes away.*) He's a rotten ignoramus.

MITCHEM: All right, that'll do. Pack it in. Now listen, all of you. We're taking this boy back to camp with us. I want to get him there in one piece.

JOHNSTONE: It's a bit dodgy, isn't it, Mitch?

MITCHEM: Happen.

JOHNSTONE: It's going to be a dodgy number as it is. You don't know how many more of them there are out there.

MITCHEM: Not yet.

JOHNSTONE: They could be coming down in strength.

MITCHEM: They might.

JOHNSTONE: And if they are we're up the creek all right. We've got enough on getting this lot back. They've no experience. We'll have to belt it like the clappers out of hell. We can't afford to hang about.

MITCHEM: We'll shift.

JOHNSTONE: But if we're going to cart a prisoner along as well . . .

MITCHEM: He'll go the pace. I'll see to that.

JOHNSTONE: You're in charge.

MITCHEM: That's right. Corporal Macleish! Smith!

MACLEISH: Sergeant?

SMITH: Sarge?

MITCHEM: I've got a job for you two. Outside. (MACLEISH *and* SMITH *exchange glances.*) I want the pair of you to nip down as far as the main track. Look for any signs of any more of them. O.K.?

MACLEISH: You want us to go down now, Sarge?

MITCHEM: Straight away. If the coast's clear we want to belt off back. Smartish.

MACLEISH: Right.

MITCHEM: Take it steady – careful – but don't make a meal out of it. The sooner we can make a start from here the better.

MACLEISH *and* SMITH *strap on their ammunition pouches.*

MACLEISH: Supposing we should . . . make contact?

MITCHEM: Don't. Not if you can help it. If you see anything that moves – turn back. Mac, you'd better take a sten. Take mine. (MACLEISH *crosses and takes sten and a couple of clips of ammunition from* MITCHEM. SMITH *unsheaths his bayonet and clips it on his rifle.*) Come on. (MITCHEM, MACLEISH *and* SMITH *cross to the door.*) What's it like out, Evans?

EVANS: Quiet. Quiet as a grave.

WHITAKER: Nothing this side, Sarge.

MITCHEM: Cover them as far as you can down the track. (EVANS *and* WHITAKER *nod.* MITCHEM *opens the door slowly and ushers* SMITH *and* MACLEISH *on to the veranda.*) Off you go.

EVANS: So long, Smudger, Jock.

MITCHEM (*closes door and crosses to where* BAMFORTH *is guarding* THE PRISONER): How's he behaving himself?

BAMFORTH (*fingering the bayonet*): All right. He hasn't got much choice.

MITCHEM (*to* THE PRISONER): You listen to me. Understand? You come with us. We take you back. We take you back with us. Oh, blimey . . . Look . . . Bamforth.

BAMFORTH: Yeh?

MITCHEM: Tell him he can drop his hands. He isn't going to run away.

BAMFORTH: Hey, Tojo! Flingers off blonce. Flingers off blonce! (THE PRISONER *raises his hands in the air.*) Not that, you nit! Here, that's not bad though, is it? He's coming on. He knows his flingers already. Good old Tojo! (THE PRISONER *smiles.*) Now let them dlop. Dlop, see! Down! (BAMFORTH *demonstrates and* THE PRISONER *slowly drops his hands.*) He picks up quick. He's a glutton for knowledge.

MITCHEM (*speaks slowly and carefully*): You – come – with – us! Back! We – take – you – back! (THE PRISONER *is mystified.*) Back to camp! (MITCHEM *turns away.*) What's the use . . . (MITCHEM *crosses to table.*)

BAMFORTH: I'll work on him. I'll chat him up a bit.

JOHNSTONE: We should have done him first time off.

MITCHEM: I'm giving the orders!

BAMFORTH: Flingers on blonce. (THE PRISONER *complies happily.*) Dlop flingers. (*Again* THE PRISONER *obeys.*) Get that! He dlops them like a two-year-old!

JOHNSTONE: Just keep him quiet, Bamforth, that's all. We don't want any of the funny patter!

BAMFORTH: I'm teaching him to talk!

JOHNSTONE: Well don't! Mitch, we've got fifteen miles to slog it back. We've got no set. We know the Japs are coming through – so someone's waiting for a report – and quick. We can't drag him along – suppose he tries to come it on? One shout from him with any of his boys around we're in the cart. The lot of us.

MITCHEM: So what do you suggest?

JOHNSTONE: Get rid of him. Right now. You going soft?

MITCHEM: And if we do? You want to make out the report when we get back?

JOHNSTONE: Report! You want to make out a report! Because we do a Jap? We whip him out and knock him off, that's all. We can't take prisoners. We're out to do a job.

MITCHEM: Reports on him don't bother me. And if I've got to do for him – I will. I'll knock him off myself. You think I'm stuffing my nut worrying about a Jap? One Jap? I've got six men. They're my responsibility. But more than that, and like you say, I've got a job to do. So all right. So I'll do it. Now you tell me what's going on out there? (MITCHEM *indicates the window.*) Just tell me how many Nips have broken through and where they are right now. You want to wait and count them for yourself?

JOHNSTONE: I want to slog it back!

MITCHEM: All right. That's what we're going to do. With him. (*Points to* THE PRISONER.) With Tojo there. Because if anybody knows the strength of Nips behind our lines it's him. So far on this outing out it's been the biggest muck-up in the history of the British Army, and that's saying a lot. We've wandered round, the set's packed in, we've no idea what's going on and if there ever was an organized shambles – my God, this is it. Now things have changed. We've copped on to a lad who's going to make this detail worth its while. If I can get him back to camp what they'll get out of him could do more good than you if you should serve a score and one. So he's important for what he knows. And I'll leave any man on this patrol behind – including you – before I'll say goodbye to him. Going soft? Do you think

I give a twopenny damn about his life? It's what he knows.

JOHNSTONE: Suppose he comes the ab-dabs on the way?

MITCHEM: He won't.

JOHNSTONE: But if he does? He only needs to start playing it up at the wrong time. He only wants to start coming it on when we're close to his muckers.

MITCHEM: I've said he won't.

JOHNSTONE: What if he does?

MITCHEM *and* JOHNSTONE *glance across at* THE PRISONER.

MITCHEM: I'll put the bayonet in his guts myself. (*Pause.*) You'd better check these Jap grenades. Might come in handy.

MITCHEM *and* JOHNSTONE *turn to table to check the grenades. The Prisoner's hand goes up to his breast pocket.* BAMFORTH *raises the bayonet threateningly.*

BAMFORTH: Watch it, Tojo boy! Just watch your step! I'll have it in as soon as look at you!

MITCHEM (*glancing round*): What's up with him?

BAMFORTH: Going for his pocket.

THE PRISONER *gestures towards his pocket.*

MITCHEM: All right. See what he wants.

BAMFORTH (*still threatening with the bayonet, he opens the Prisoner's breast pocket and takes out a cheap leather wallet*): It's his wallet.

JOHNSTONE: Sling it out the window.

MITCHEM: Let him have it. Check it first.

BAMFORTH *briefly inspects the interior of the wallet.*

JOHNSTONE: You're going to let him have it!

MITCHEM: It costs us nothing. No point in getting him niggly before we start.

BAMFORTH: Looks all right, Sarge.

MITCHEM: Give it him.

BAMFORTH *hands the wallet to* THE PRISONER, *who opens it, extracts a couple of photographs and hands one to* BAMFORTH.

BAMFORTH: It's a photo! It's a picture of a Nippo bint! (THE

PRISONER *points proudly to himself.*) Who's this, then, eh? You got wife? Your missis? (THE PRISONER *points again to himself.*) It's his old woman! Very good. Japanese girl very good, eh? Good old Tojo! She's a bit short in the pins, that's all. But very nice. (THE PRISONER *passes another photograph to* BAMFORTH.) Here! Get this! Nippo snappers, Sarge. Two Jap kids. Couple of chicos. You got two chicos, eh? (THE PRISONER *does not understand.* BAMFORTH *points to photograph and holds up two fingers.*) Two! See? You got two kids. (THE PRISONER *shakes his head and holds up three fingers.*) Three? No, you stupid raving imbecile! Two! (BAMFORTH *points again to the photograph.*) One and one's two! Dinky-doo-number-two! (THE PRISONER *holds up his hands to indicate a baby.*) What another? Another one as well! Well, you crafty old devil! You're as bad as Smudge. (BAMFORTH *returns the photographs to* THE PRISONER, *who replaces them carefully in his wallet and returns it to his pocket.*) Let's see if you still know your lessons. Flingers up on blonce! (THE PRISONER *complies.*) Dlop flingers! (*Again* THE PRISONER *is happy to obey.*) Stroll on! See that! He got it right both times! He's almost human this one is!

MITCHEM: All right, Bamforth, jack it in!

JOHNSTONE: We should have done him when he first turned up.

MITCHEM (*crossing to* EVANS): Where have them two got to?

EVANS: No sign yet, Sarge.

MITCHEM *peers out of window.* BAMFORTH *takes out a packet of cigarettes and puts one in his mouth. He replaces the packet in his pocket and feels for a box of matches as his glance falls on* THE PRISONER, *who is looking up at him.* BAMFORTH *hesitates, then transfers the cigarette from his own mouth to the Prisoner's. He takes out another cigarette for himself.* JOHNSTONE *rises and crosses to* BAMFORTH. BAMFORTH *is still looking for a match as* JOHNSTONE *takes out a box, strikes one and offers* BAMFORTH *a light.*

BAMFORTH: Ta. (JOHNSTONE *holds out the match for* THE PRISONER. *As* THE PRISONER *leans across to get a light,* JOHNSTONE *knocks the cigarette from his mouth with the back of his hand.*) What's that in aid of!

JOHNSTONE: He gets permission first!

BAMFORTH: I gave him it!

JOHNSTONE: Since when have you been calling out the time!

BAMFORTH: I don't ask you before I give a bloke a fag!

JOHNSTONE: This one you do!

BAMFORTH: Who says!

JOHNSTONE: I do, lad! (*Making a sudden grab for* THE PRISONER *and attempting to tear open his breast pocket.*) I'll fix his photos for the Herb as well!

MITCHEM (*turns*): Corporal Johnstone!

BAMFORTH (*drops the bayonet and clutches* JOHNSTONE *by his jacket lapels. He brings his knee up in Johnstone's groin and, as* JOHNSTONE *doubles forward,* BAMFORTH *cracks his forehead across the bridge of Johnstone's nose*): Have that!

MITCHEM (*crossing towards the fight*): Bamforth!

BAMFORTH, *unheeding, strikes* JOHNSTONE *in the stomach and pushes him to the floor.*

JOHNSTONE (*pulling himself to his feet*): All right. You've done it this time, Bamforth! You've shot your load. As sure as God you'll get three years for that.

BAMFORTH (*picks up bayonet*): You try and make it stick.

MITCHEM: You're on a charge, Bamforth. You're under open arrest.

BAMFORTH: He started it!

MITCHEM: Tell that to the C.O.

EVANS (*raising his rifle*): Sarge! There's someone coming up the track!

MITCHEM (*crosses to window*): Whereabouts?

EVANS: Just coming through the trees.

JOHNSTONE *picks up his sten and crosses to join* WHITAKER.

MITCHEM: It's all right. It's Macleish and Smith. Cover them up the track.

JOHNSTONE (*aiming the sten*): I've got them.

EVANS: Looks as if they're in a hurry over something.

A pause before we hear MACLEISH *and* SMITH *clatter up on to the veranda.* MITCHEM *opens the door and they enter the room. They lean against the wall exhausted.*

MITCHEM: Anybody after you? (MACLEISH *shakes his head.*) What's up then?

EVANS: What's the hurry, Smudger boy? You look as if you've had the whole of the Japanese army on your tail.

SMITH (*out of breath*): We have . . . Near enough.

MITCHEM: Sit down a tick. (SMITH *and* MACLEISH *cross to the table and sit down.* MITCHEM *crosses to join them.*) Now, come on – give. Let's be having it.

MACLEISH (*regaining his breath*): They've broken through. In strength. There's hundreds of them moving down the main trail back.

MITCHEM: Go on.

SMITH: They must have come through our defence lines like a dose of salts. They're pouring down. Happy as a lot of sand boys. Not a mark on any one of them. Up front the whole damn shoot's collapsed.

MITCHEM: You weren't spotted?

MACLEISH (*shakes his head*): They're not even looking for anybody. They seem to know they've got this area to themselves. Smudge and myself got down in the long grass. They've got no scouts out. Nothing. Just strolling down the trail as if they owned the jungle . . .

MITCHEM: Do you think they'll find this place?

MACLEISH: Not yet a while. We watched about a company march past. There was a break then in the file. We managed to cover up the entrance of the trail up here.

SMITH: We stuffed it up with bits of branch and stuff.

MITCHEM: Good.

MACLEISH: The next batch came along as we were finishing. We patched up what we could and scooted back.

JOHNSTONE: So what happens now?

MITCHEM: It's put the kybosh on the journey back. We can't move out of here just yet, and that's a certainty.

MACLEISH: You never saw so many Japs. There must be at least a thousand of them now between ourselves and base. We're right behind their forward lines.

MITCHEM (*crosses downstage and turns*): Let's say, for now, they march without a stop. That brings them close up on the camp before tomorrow night. If they've got stuff up in the air to back them up – and if they don't know back at base they've broken through – the base mob gets wiped up.

MACLEISH: But they'll know by now the Japs are through.

MITCHEM: We can't count on that.

JOHNSTONE: If the main road's free, they'll have heavy transport loads of Nips chugging down before tomorrow.

MITCHEM: Let's hope the Engineers have sewn that up. They'll have it mined at least. No, this is the back way in. Cross country – and it's hard graft cutting trail – they'll have to do the lot on foot.

JOHNSTONE: So?

MITCHEM: So that means we can put the blocks on them. We get there first.

JOHNSTONE: You think the Japs are going to open ranks and let us pass?

MITCHEM: What's the time now? (*He glances at his watch.*) It'll be dark in just over an hour. We might make it then.

JOHNSTONE: And so you think we stand a chance at creeping through a regiment of ruddy Nips!

MITCHEM: What's your suggestion?

JOHNSTONE: We haven't got a chance.

MITCHEM: We've got no choice. We might make it in the dark and in that shrub. They'll be blundering about themselves. At least we know the way – we've done it coming up.

It's all new ground to them. We might creep through.

JOHNSTONE (*indicating* THE PRISONER): What? With him in tow?

MITCHEM (*glancing across at* THE PRISONER): No . . . We're ditching him. Whitaker!

WHITAKER (*turning at window*): Sarge?

MITCHEM (*indicating set*): Come on. You'd better give it one more try.

WHITAKER: I don't think it'll do any good, Sarge. The battery's nigh on stone dead.

MITCHEM: Try it, lad! Don't argue. Relieve him, Smith.

SMITH *crosses to take Whitaker's place at the window as* WHITAKER *crosses to table and sits at set. He switches on to 'transmit' and pauses.*

MITCHEM: Come on, lad! Get on with it! We haven't time to mess about.

WHITAKER (*turning in his chair to speak to* MITCHEM): If there are any Japs near here switched to receive they'll get a fix on us.

MITCHEM: That can't be helped. Come on, come on!

WHITAKER (*putting on headphones and tuning in*): Blue Patrol to Red Leader . . . Blue Patrol to Red Leader . . . Are you receiving me? . . . Are you receiving me? . . . Come in Red Leader . . . Come in Red Leader . . . Over . . . (WHITAKER *switches to 'receive' and tunes in. We hear the crackle of interference.*) Nothing yet . . .

MITCHEM: Come on, Sammy son, come on . . .

WHITAKER (*adjusting tuning dial*): There's something here . . . (*The interference dies away and we hear the voice of the Japanese radio operator as before.*) It's the Jap transmitting, Same as before.

MITCHEM: Get off the ruddy line, you Nip!

The voice continues in Japanese for a few seconds and then stops. It continues in taunting broken English.

OPERATOR: Johnnee! . . . Johnnee! . . . British Johnnee! We –

you – come – to – get . . . We – you – come – to – get.

WHITAKER *starts up in fear and* MITCHEM *pushes him back into his chair. The patrol turn and look at* THE PRISONER. THE PRISONER, *noting that all attention is centred on himself, and feeling that he is expected to entertain the patrol, raises his hands in the air and slowly places them on his head. He smiles round blandly in search of approbation.*

THE CURTAIN FALLS

ACT TWO

Time: Thirty minutes later.

As the curtain rises we discover BAMFORTH, EVANS *and* JOHN-
STONE *asleep on the ground by the wall, Left,* MACLEISH *is
guarding* THE PRISONER, *who is still sitting on the form where
we left him.* SMITH *and* WHITAKER *are standing at the rear
windows.* MITCHEM *is seated at the table cleaning his sten. A
bird sings out in the jungle and* WHITAKER *starts and raises his
rifle. He realizes the cause of his fears and glances round the
room in embarrassment. The other occupants, however, have not
noticed this lapse on the part of* WHITAKER. MITCHEM *places
his sten on the table and crosses to* SMITH.

MITCHEM: All O.K., Smudge?

SMITH: All O.K.

MITCHEM: Sammy?

WHITAKER: Nothing to report here, Sarnt. What time is it
now?

MITCHEM (*glances at his watch*): 'Bout quarter past. (*He returns
to his task at the table.*)

SMITH: Why don't you buy a watch?

WHITAKER: I had one, Smudger. Bought one down the town
once. When I had a week-end off one time. Twenty-eight
bucks it was. A good one.

SMITH: Twenty-eight! For a watch? They saw you coming,
and no mistake.

WHITAKER: No, man, it was a good one, I tell you. Smasher.
Told you the date and what day it was and all that. Little
red jewels for numbers and a sort of little moon came up
to tell you when it's night.

SMITH: You can see when it's night. It gets dark.

WHITAKER: Aye, but it was a smashing watch, Smudge. You can't get watches like that one was in Blighty. There was a bloke in the N.A.A.F.I. offered me forty bucks for it once. Forty bucks and a sort of Siamese ring he was wearing.

SMITH: You took it?

WHITAKER: I turned it down.

SMITH: What for?

WHITAKER: I'm not a fool altogether. You wouldn't get another watch like that. I was going to give it to the old man as a present when we get back home. I wouldn't have minded the ring, though. That was a beauty. Peruvian gold.

SMITH: I thought you said it was Siamese?

WHITAKER: It was. It had a kind of Siamese bint on the front. Doing a sort of dance with her knees bent in front of a temple – her hands sticking up in the air.

SMITH: So where is it?

WHITAKER: It wouldn't come off his finger.

SMITH: I mean the watch.

WHITAKER: I wasn't going to swop the watch for that, boy. I've got more sense than that. I could have flogged it for a fortune back in Blighty – if I hadn't have been going to give it to the old man for his present.

SMITH: So where is it then?

WHITAKER: I lost it. Well, it got knocked off. It was half-inched back in camp. I left it in the ablutions one morning while I went off to the latrine. I wasn't gone above two minutes – it was about the time they were giving us fruit salad twice a day and dehydrated spuds. When I came back it was gone. Two minutes at the most. My tooth-paste was gone as well. That was the most expensive trot to the lav that I ever had, I know that. Boy, there's some thieving rascals round the camp.

SMITH: You should have reported it to the R.S.M. Had a personal kit inspection.

WHITAKER: Ah, what would have been the use? I wouldn't have got it back. If anybody pinched a watch like that he wouldn't leave it lying around in his locker, man. He'd want his head looking at. I've never bought another one since then. I haven't had the heart for it. What time did you say it was, Sarnt?

MITCHEM: I've just told you.

WHITAKER: I forgot.

MITCHEM: Quarter past.

WHITAKER: Roll on. Roll on my relief and let me get my head down. Sergeant Mitchem?

MITCHEM: What is it? What's up now?

WHITAKER: What time we setting off?

MITCHEM: I'll tell you. When it's time to move. We won't leave you behind. Don't worry. No need to flap.

    WHITAKER, *who has been talking to take his mind off other things, relapses into silence.*

MITCHEM (*takes out his water bottle and has a drink. He glances across at* THE PRISONER *and hands the water bottle to* MACLEISH): Here, Jock, see'f Noisy Harry wants a gob.

MACLEISH: Right, Sarge. (MACLEISH *offers the water bottle to* THE PRISONER, *who accepts it gratefully.* THE PRISONER *takes two pulls at the bottle, wipes the mouth, recorks it and hands it back to* MACLEISH *who, in turn, returns it to* MITCHEM.) Your bottle.

MITCHEM (*glances up from cleaning the sten as* MACLEISH *places the water bottle on the table*): Right. Thanks.

MACLEISH (*anxious to start a conversation*): He doesn't seem a bad sort of bloke.

MITCHEM: Who? Him?

MACLEISH: I suppose there's good and bad wherever you look. I mean, he's quiet enough.

MITCHEM: What did you expect?

MACLEISH: Oh, I don't know . . . You hear these tales. I suppose it is all over? Up country, I mean?

MITCHEM: You saw them coming through, lad.

MACLEISH: Aye. Only I was wondering if they'd taken many prisoners themselves. The Japs, I mean.

MITCHEM: Search me.

MACLEISH: It seems to me . . . I've been thinking it over, like, in my mind. And I was thinking, at the little time it's taken them to get down here – as far as this – they couldn't have had a lot of resistance. I mean, do you think it's possible there's been a sort of general jacking in from our lads?

MITCHEM: Happen. I don't know.

MACLEISH: I mean, if there'd been anything like a scrap at all they'd still be at it now, if you see what I mean.

MITCHEM: It follows. They might be still at it, for all we know. Mopping up. We don't know how much of the front still stands – if any. It could be just a section of the line packed in.

MACLEISH: I was wondering about Donald – that's my brother.

MITCHEM: Yeh?

MACLEISH: Well, if you work on the assumption that it's all over – that they've come straight through . . .

MITCHEM: It doesn't do to count on 'ifs' in this lark.

MACLEISH: No. But if they have, it's likely that they've copped a lot of prisoners, the Japs. That stands to reason.

MITCHEM: That's fair enough.

MACLEISH: So it's possible my brother is a P.O.W. already.

MITCHEM: There's a chance of that.

MACLEISH: You hear so many stories – you know, on how the Japs treat P.O.W.s.

MITCHEM: Pretty rough, they reckon.

MACLEISH: I'm not so sure. You hear all kinds of things. As if they're almost . . . animals. But this bloke seems a decent sort of bloke.

MITCHEM: It's hard to tell.

MACLEISH: I mean, he's a family man himself.

MITCHEM: So what? Is that supposed to make a difference?

MACLEISH: He's human at least.

MITCHEM: What do you want for your money? Dracula? Look, son, forget the home and family bull. You put a bloke in uniform and push him overseas and he's a different bloke to what he was before. I've watched it happen scores of times.

MACLEISH: But if a bloke's got a wife and family himself . . .

MITCHEM: You get a bloke between your sights and stop to wonder if he's got a family, Jock, your family's not got you. There's half of them got families and most of them are nigs like us who don't know why we're here or what it's all in aid of. It's not your worry that. You're not paid to think.

MACLEISH: I used to wonder . . . Worried me a lot . . . I've often wondered, if it came to the push, was it inside me to kill a man.

MITCHEM: It's inside all of us. That's the trouble. Just needs fetching out, and some need more to bring it out than others.

MACLEISH: You know – when we got this one – when he first came in – I couldn't do it. I just couldn't move. I don't know now whether I'm sorry or I'm glad.

MITCHEM: You'll do it if it's necessary.

MACLEISH: I'm not worried, mind. I mean, I'm not afraid or anything like that. At least, I don't think I'm afraid no more than anybody else. I think if it was outside it would be different. The way you look at things, I mean. If it was him or me. Something moving about in the trees – something you can put a bullet in and not have to . . . have to look into its eyes.

MITCHEM: I've told you once – you think too much. Outside or else in here – what's the difference?

MACLEISH: Outside he's got a fighting chance.

MITCHEM: Don't come that. It's not a game of darts. You can't wipe the board clean and start all over again. Mugs away. The mugs have had it. There are far too many mugs about. We're all mugs, and I'll tell you why. I'll tell you what's the trouble with this world, Jock – bints.

MACLEISH (*amused*): Go on!

MITCHEM: It's right. Straight up. They cause more upset than enough. Half the scrapping in this world is over judies. There's half the blokes out here now who'd be sitting back in Blighty still with wangled home postings if it wasn't for a bint. It's bints who go a bundle over uniforms. You take a bloke – an ordinary bloke who gets called up. He doesn't want to go. He doesn't want to come out here, or if he does he's round the bend. Then, one day, this poor Charlie winds up with a bird – it happens to us all in the end. She whips him up the dancers once and that's the end of that. She likes the colour of his uniform and that makes him feel big. Six months before he was sitting behind a desk, copping on a weekly, picking his nose and chatting up the pigeons on the window-sill. Now – all at once – he feels like he's a man. Before he knows where he is he's standing on the boat deck and the bint's waving him off from the docks with a bitsy hanky and tears clogging up her powder. My hero stuff. The captain blows the whistle on the bridge. The gang-plank's up. There's a military band on the quay-side, best boots and battledress, playing 'Where was the Engine Driver?' 'Goodbye Dolly I must leave you.' So there stands Charlie Harry, five foot four in his socks, and feeling like he's Clive of India, Alexander the Great and Henry Five rolled into one.

MACLEISH: You're a real one for handing out the patter.

MITCHEM: Few weeks after that he's on his back with his feet in the air and a hole as big as your fist in his belly. And he's nothing.

MACLEISH (*uneasily*): I reckon that it's you who thinks too much.

MITCHEM: I'm not a thinking kind of man. I look at facts. It happens to us all. Do you think that bint is going to float off to a nunnery? (*Indicating* THE PRISONER.) Just take a look at him. For all you know, his missis back in Tokyo thinks he's a sort of Rudolph Valentino.

MACLEISH: If she does she wants glasses.

MITCHEM: Happen so. But that's the way it is. So just you drop the home and bint and family bull. You might end up like him.

MACLEISH: How's that?

MITCHEM: What do you mean?

MACLEISH: So how does he end up when we head back?

MITCHEM: We're stacking him.

MACLEISH: That's what I understood. You mean we're leaving him behind.

MITCHEM: It's a sticky number as it is. We've got to go right through the lot of them. We'd never make it with a prisoner as well. It's odds against us now. With him as well we wouldn't stand a chance.

MACLEISH: I was beginning to get quite fond of him.

MITCHEM: He's no use now. He couldn't tell us any more than we know already. He's no cop to us. He's lost his value.

MACLEISH: Are we going to leave him here?

MITCHEM: Yeh.

MACLEISH: In the hut?

MITCHEM: That's right.

MACLEISH: That's a bit risky, isn't it?

MITCHEM: How do you mean?

MACLEISH: Suppose they find the track up here? Suppose the Japs come up and cut him loose? He lets them know what time we left. How many there are of us.

MITCHEM: He won't.

MACLEISH: Aye, but if he did? If they knew how much start

we had on them they'd catch us up in no time. If he could tell them that . . .

MITCHEM: He won't.

MACLEISH: There's nothing to stop him.

MITCHEM: I've told you twice, he won't!

MACLEISH: I mean, it seems to me the risk's as big as if we tried to take him back with us. They know we're somewhere in this area. It's only a matter of time before they find this place.

MITCHEM: They don't know anything.

MACLEISH: They know we're round about here somewhere. Why else would they be bashing out the patter on the set?

MITCHEM: It's regular procedure with the Nips. Routine stuff. They push out muck in English on the off-chance. To put the wind up anyone who might be hanging round. It doesn't mean a thing.

MACLEISH: We won't have time to cover up the entrance of the track again. We'll have to go straight through. I mean, the path up here is going to be wide open. It's going to be like putting up a sign. The minute we move out of here it's ten to one they'll find the track straight off.

MITCHEM: They'll find him, that's all.

MACLEISH: Aye. But he can tell them. About us.

MITCHEM: He won't tell anybody. Anything.

MACLEISH: What's to stop him?

MITCHEM: I'll see to that.

MACLEISH: I fail to see what you can do about it.

MITCHEM: You don't have to.

MACLEISH: You're not . . . you're not going to knock him off?

MITCHEM: Just you do your job, Mac, that's all.

MACLEISH: You're not going to knock him off!

MITCHEM: Do you want to do it?

MACLEISH: He's a P.O.W.!

MITCHEM: Shut up.

MACLEISH: You can't kill him!

MITCHEM: That's my worry.

MACLEISH: The man's a prisoner-of-war!

MITCHEM: There's thousands more like him between this mob and base. It's him that's playing at home today, not you and me. If anybody's P.O.W.s it's us – not him.

MACLEISH: He gave himself up.

MITCHEM: He should have had more sense.

MACLEISH: You can't just walk him outside and put a bullet into him.

MITCHEM: No. I know that. It'd make too much noise.

MACLEISH (*glancing down at the bayonet he holds in his hand*): Oh, God . . . Not that.

MITCHEM: Do you think I'm looking forward to it?

MACLEISH: Not that . . . Not like that.

MITCHEM: I've got six men and one report to come out of this lot. If I hang on to him it could work out I lose the whole patrol. I could lose more than that. For all we know, the unit's sitting back on its backside with thousands of these little Harries streaming down in that direction. You reckon I should lose my sleep over him?

MACLEISH: There must be something else.

MITCHEM: There isn't.

MACLEISH: There's another way.

MITCHEM: It's no good!

MACLEISH: Suppose we tied him up and ditched him in the bushes. Round the back, say. Out of sight. So it took a while for them to find him.

MITCHEM: It's no good.

MACLEISH: It's a damn sight better than doing him in.

MITCHEM: Is that what you think? Use your head. Do you think I haven't thought of that already? We hide him up out here he starves to death. That could take days. Do you think that's doing him a favour?

MACLEISH: What do you think you're doing?

MITCHEM: Me? My job. What they pay me to do.

MACLEISH: To knock off P.O.W.s!

MITCHEM: To put first things first.

MACLEISH: It's bloody murder, man!

MITCHEM (*crossing to* MACLEISH): 'Course it is. That is my job. That's why I'm here. And you. (*He indicates his stripes.*) That's why I'm wearing these. And I'm wearing these 'cause I'm the one that makes decisions. Like this. If you want to do that, Jock, you can have my job right now. Here and now. It stinks. To me, it stinks. It stinks to me to do for him. But, come to that, the whole lot stinks to me. So what am I supposed to do? Turn conshi? Jack it in? Leave the world to his lot?

MACLEISH: I've got a brother who could just be sitting back – right now. Like him.

MITCHEM: Jock, I can smell your kind a mile away.

MACLEISH: What's that supposed to mean?

MITCHEM: The Bamforth touch.

MACLEISH: Bammo?

MITCHEM: You're as bad as Bamforth, boy.

MACLEISH: Me! You think that I'm like Bamforth?

MITCHEM: All the bloody way.

MACLEISH: You're off your nut.

MITCHEM: It's the book. According to the book. You can't forget the book. All along the road – the book. It doesn't work. You'd make a right pair. Nothing to choose between you – except that Bammo fiddles it to suit himself. You like to come the greater glory of mankind.

MACLEISH: It seems to me you're talking out of the back of your head.

MITCHEM: Don't you believe it. And to think that it was me who put you up for that tape. You're right – I must be going round the bend.

MACLEISH: You can strip me when you want. You know what you can do with the tape.

MITCHEM: And wouldn't that be lovely, eh? Wouldn't that just suit you down to the ground?

MACLEISH: How's that?

MITCHEM: It lets you out of this. On the ground floor. You're back in the ranks. One of the boys and none of the responsibility.

MACLEISH: Perhaps I'd rather be one of the boys.

MITCHEM: You can say that again. So why did you cop on for the tape in the first place?

MACLEISH: I've never complained about doing my job – that doesn't mean I'm willing to be a party to what you're suggesting.

MITCHEM: Lad, have you got lots to learn. How did you reckon it was going to be? Like in the comics? Fearless Mac Macleish charging up a little hill with a score of grenades and highland war cries? Wiping out machine-guns single-handed? The gallant lance-jack gutting half a dozen Nips with a Boy Scout penknife and a Union Jack? Walking back to Jock-land with enough medals to sink a destroyer?

MACLEISH: You're talking through your hat.

MITCHEM (*crossing to* MACLEISH): Yeh? Reckon, do you? Happen so. Perhaps you're right. You happen haven't got the guts for that. I'll tell you this much, boy – a touch like that's the easiest thing on earth. The army's full of square-head yobs who keep their brains between their legs. Blokes who do their nuts for fifteen seconds and cop a decoration, cheer boys cheer, Rule Britannia and death before dishonour. All right. Why not? Good luck to them. Lads like that win wars so they should have the medals. They deserve them. But a touch like this comes harder. The trouble is with war – a lot of it's like this – most of it. Too much. You've that to learn.

MACLEISH: There's nothing you can teach me.

MITCHEM: You're dead right there.

MACLEISH: I make my own decisions.

MITCHEM: It's the only way. I'll just say this much, Jock: before you get much older you'll grow up. If this war shapes the way I think it will, you'll grow up, lad, in next to no time. (*He crosses towards table.*) Before the month is out you'll do a dozen jobs like this before you have your breakfast. (*He sits at table.*) So just think on.

WHITAKER (*turning at window*): Sergeant Mitchem.

MITCHEM: You again? What is it now?

WHITAKER: I . . . I was wondering what the time was now.

MITCHEM: Not again! What's up? Do you want changing?

WHITAKER: It was just that I was wondering what time it was.

MITCHEM (*glances at his watch*): Half-past – all but.

WHITAKER: I thought it must be getting on that way.

MITCHEM: Another minute and I'll give the lads a shout.

    THE PRISONER *gestures towards his breast pocket.*

MACLEISH: Sarnt . . . Sergeant Mitchem!

MITCHEM (*glancing round*): I ought to change my name. What's your complaint?

MACLEISH: It's him. I think there's something that he wants.

MITCHEM: If it's outside he can't. Tell him to hold it.

MACLEISH: Something in his pocket.

MITCHEM: Again? Oh – all right. O.K. See what it is. You get it for him.

MACLEISH: Right (*To* THE PRISONER) Now, you behave yourself, my lad. (MACLEISH *opens the Prisoner's breast pocket and extracts the wallet.*) Is it this? (THE PRISONER *shakes his head.* MACLEISH *replaces the wallet and takes a cigarette case from the Prisoner's pocket.*) Is this it? Is it this that you were wanting? (THE PRISONER *nods his head.*) Is it all right for the prisoner to have a drag, Sarge?

MITCHEM: Yeh. O.K.

MACLEISH (*he hands the case to* THE PRISONER *who takes out two cigarettes, offering one to* MACLEISH): Who? Me? You're giving one to me? (*He takes the proffered cigarette.* THE PRISONER *closes the case and places it on the form.*) That's

... that's very kind of you. (MACLEISH *takes a box of matches from his pocket.*) My name's Macleish. (*Points to himself.*) Macleish. Do you understand? (*Pointing again to himself.*) Macleish – me (*He points to* THE PRISONER.) Who – are – you? (THE PRISONER *places his hands on his head.*) Is that the only thing you know?

MITCHEM (*crosses towards the sleeping figures of* BAMFORTH, EVANS *and* JOHNSTONE): I shouldn't get too attached to him. (*He shakes* JOHNSTONE.) Johnno! ... Johnno!

    MACLEISH *gives* THE PRISONER *a light behind following dialogue.*

JOHNSTONE (*wakes and sits up*): Yeh?

MITCHEM: Half-past.

JOHNSTONE (*rubs his eyes*): Right.

MITCHEM (*crosses and shakes* BAMFORTH): Come on, come on! Wakey-wakey, rise and shine. Let's have you! (BAMFORTH *sits up as* MITCHEM *crosses to wake* EVANS.) Evans! Evans, lad!

EVANS (*sitting up*): I feel horrible.

MITCHEM: You look it. Get your skates on. Let's be having you. The sun's burning your eyes out. Move yourselves, then!

EVANS: What's the time, Sarnt?

MITCHEM: Don't you start that as well. It's turned half-past. (*He crosses to table and sits down, then glances across at* BAMFORTH *and* EVANS, *who have not, as yet, made any attempt to rise.*) Come on! I said, move yourselves!

BAMFORTH: I've got a mouth like the inside of a tram driver's glove.

EVANS: Had a good kip, Bammo boy?

BAMFORTH: What? Kipping next to you? Kipping with a Taff? How could I? (*He lights a cigarette.*) I was having a smashing dream, though, son.

EVANS: Who was she?

BAMFORTH: Why should I tell you – you dream about your own. You dream about the milk-maids, Taff. They're more in your line. Have a sordid nightmare. The bints in my dreams have got class. Society bints.

EVANS: I bet they are.

BAMFORTH: Straight up.

JOHNSTONE: What do you know about society bints, Bamforth?

BAMFORTH: All the lot. You have to kiss them first.

   EVANS *laughs.*

JOHNSTONE (*now on his feet*): Got all the answers, haven't you?

BAMFORTH: Most of them. You've got to have with bints.

MITCHEM: All right, less of the love life, Bamforth. Let's have you on your feet.

BAMFORTH *and* EVANS *rise and adjust their uniforms as* JOHNSTONE *crosses to the table.*

JOHNSTONE: Anything fresh?

MITCHEM (*shakes his head*): Not yet. We haven't tried the set again. Nothing new outside. (*He glances up as* BAMFORTH *crosses towards the door.*) What you on, then?

BAMFORTH (*at door*): I want to go outside!

MITCHEM: What for?

BAMFORTH: I can't help it.

MITCHEM: I don't want anybody moving round outside.

BAMFORTH: It's not my fault!

MITCHEM: All right. Go on. And make it sharp.

BAMFORTH (*to* SMITH): So what am I supposed to do? Write out an application?

MITCHEM: If you're going, Bamforth, you'd better get off now.

BAMFORTH (*opens door*): All right! (*To* SMITH.) So long.

EVANS (*crossing to stand by* SMITH): Bring me back a coconut, boy!

BAMFORTH (*as he exits*): Fetch your own.

MITCHEM: Whitaker!

WHITAKER (*turning at window*): Sarge?

MITCHEM: Cover him outside.

WHITAKER: Righto.

JOHNSTONE: What time we pushing off?

MITCHEM: Another half an hour, happen. Maybe more. As soon as it gets dark enough to give us cover.

JOHNSTONE (*inclining his head towards* THE PRISONER): And him?

MITCHEM: It's settled what we're going to do with him.

JOHNSTONE (*takes out a packet of cigarettes and offers one to* MITCHEM): Who?

MITCHEM (*shakes his head, declining the cigarette*): Meaning what?

JOHNSTONE (*lights his own cigarette before answering*): Who gets to do the job?

MITCHEM: Are you volunteering?

JOHNSTONE (*blows out a cloud of smoke*): I don't mind.

MITCHEM: Do you know, I think you would at that.

JOHNSTONE: Somebody's got to do it.

MITCHEM: It's got to be arranged yet, has that. We could draw lots. I don't know – perhaps I ought to do the job myself.

JOHNSTONE: It wants doing quick.

MITCHEM: I know.

JOHNSTONE: And quiet.

MITCHEM: I know.

JOHNSTONE: It's a skilled job.

MITCHEM: I know all that!

JOHNSTONE: So it wants somebody who knows what they're doing. You or me. We could toss up.

MITCHEM: Look – don't try and teach me my job, eh?

JOHNSTONE: Only trying to help. Just making a suggestion. It wants a professional touch. (*He glances across at* THE PRISONER *who is still smoking.*) Who gave him that?

MITCHEM: You what?

JOHNSTONE (*crosses and grasps the Prisoner's wrist*): Macleish!

Have you been keeping him in smokes?

MITCHEM: I gave him permission.

JOHNSTONE (*releasing the Prisoner's hand in disgust*): All right. Carry on.

MACLEISH: I didn't give him the fag, in any case. (*He indicates his own cigarette.*) As a matter of fact, it was him who gave me this.

JOHNSTONE: Going mates already?

MACLEISH: 'Course not.

JOHNSTONE: What's up then? Do you fancy him?

MACLEISH: I can't see that there's any harm in accepting a fag from the bloke.

JOHNSTONE: You wouldn't.

MACLEISH: There's no harm in that!

JOHNSTONE: Not much. You ought to go the whole way, lad. Turn native. You'll be eating your connor from banana leaves next. I wouldn't touch his stinking wog tobacco.

MACLEISH: It's just an ordinary cigarette.

JOHNSTONE: You what? Let's have a shufti.

MACLEISH (*holding up his cigarette for Johnstone's inspection*): It's just the same as any other cigarette. There's no difference.

JOHNSTONE (*taking the cigarette from* MACLEISH): You wouldn't chuckle. It's the same all right. There's not a bit of difference. It's a Blighty fag. (*He snatches the cigarette from* THE PRISONER.) They're British smokes. They're British army issue!

MITCHEM (*rising and crossing to join* JOHNSTONE): Give us hold. (JOHNSTONE *hands one of the cigarettes to* MITCHEM, *who examines it closely.*) They're army issue right enough. He must have thieved them from the lads up country.

MITCHEM, MACLEISH *and* JOHNSTONE *turn and look at* THE PRISONER.

EVANS (*crossing to join the group*): What's the matter, Jock? What's happened?

MACLEISH: It's him. It's bright boy there. He's carrying a load of British issue fags.

EVANS: How did he get hold of them?

JOHNSTONE: How do you think? You can have three guesses. The thieving Nip!

MITCHEM (*drops the cigarette and grinds it beneath his heel*): If there's one thing gets my hump it's knocking off – it's looting.

JOHNSTONE (*holding out the cigarette to* MACLEISH): Well, come on, Jock, you'd better finish it. You're the one he gave it to. You reckon you're his mate.

MACLEISH (*snatching the cigarette*): I'll ram it down his rotten throat! I'll make him eat the rotten thing! (*He hesitates – for a moment we feel that he is about to carry out the threat – he hurls the cigarette across the room.*)

JOHNSTONE: You don't want to waste it. Jock. Not now you've started it. You never know how much that fag has cost. He's happen stuck his bayonet end in some poor Herb for that.

EVANS: There's some of them would kill their mothers for a drag.

MITCHEM (*to* MACLEISH): And you were telling me how they treat P.O.W.s.

EVANS: He wants a lesson, Sarge. He ought to have a lesson taught to him.

MACLEISH: I'll kill him!

MITCHEM: Will you? You swop sides quick. (*There is a pause as they turn to look at* THE PRISONER, *who, uncertain of their attitude towards him, picks up the case, opens it and offers a cigarette to* MITCHEM.) Stick 'em! (MITCHEM *strikes the case from the Prisoner's hand.* THE PRISONER *raises his hands and places them on his head – on this occasion, however, the action is without humour.*) Thieving slob!

JOHNSTONE (*raising a fist*): Who goes in first?

MITCHEM: Hold it.

JOHNSTONE (*advancing threateningly on* THE PRISONER): Who gets first crack?

MITCHEM: Hold it a sec!

> JOHNSTONE *checks himself.*

MACLEISH (*almost to himself*): My brother's just nineteen. He's only been out here a couple of months. I haven't seen him since he docked. They whipped him straight up country. He's only just nineteen. (*A loud appeal to the patrol – as if in the hope of receiving a denial.*) For all I know he's dead!

MITCHEM: Jock – see'f he's lugging anything else he's lifted from our lads.

MACLEISH (*moving to* THE PRISONER): Get up! Get on your feet! (THE PRISONER *cowers on the form and* MACLEISH *jerks him savagely to his feet.*) Do as you're told! (MACLEISH *goes through the Prisoner's pocket and removes the wallet.*) There's this.

JOHNSTONE (*taking the wallet*): I'll have a look at what's in this. You carry on.

MACLEISH (*as* THE PRISONER *reacts slightly at the loss of the wallet*): Stand still!

MACLEISH *goes through the Prisoner's trouser pockets and removes the usual miscellaneous assortment of articles: handkerchief, keys, loose change, etc.* MACLEISH *places these on the form.* JOHNSTONE, *slowly and carefully, tears the photographs into pieces and drops these and the wallet on the floor.* THE PRISONER *starts forward and* MACLEISH *rises and strikes him across the face.* BAMFORTH, *who has just re-entered from the veranda, notices this incident.*

MACLEISH: I said, stand still!

BAMFORTH: What's up? What's he done to ask for that?

EVANS: He's been looting, Bammo. From our lads.

BAMFORTH (*crossing to join the group around* THE PRISONER): He's been what?

MACLEISH: We caught him with a fag-case stuffed with British army smokes.

BAMFORTH: You Scotch nit! You dim Scotch nit! I gave
    him them!

MITCHEM: You did?

BAMFORTH: I'm telling you. I gave him half a dozen snouts!

EVANS: You gave them him?

    MACLEISH *edges away from* THE PRISONER *and* BAM-
FORTH *positions himself between* THE PRISONER *and the*
members of the patrol.

BAMFORTH: What's the matter, Taff? Are your ears bad?
    I slipped him half a dozen nubs!

MACLEISH: I didn't know. I thought . . . I thought he'd
    knocked them off.

JOHNSTONE (*to* BAMFORTH): And who gave you permission?

BAMFORTH: I've had this out with you before. You show
    where it says I have to grease up to an N.C.O. before I
    hand out fags. What's mine's my own. I decide what I do
    with it.

MACLEISH: How was I to know? I . . . I've told you, boy, I
    thought he'd knocked them off.

BAMFORTH: You know what thought did.

MACLEISH (*searching for words*): How was I to know? . . .
    I mean, he gave one of them to me . . . I'd lit it up . . . I was
    having a drag . . . I was half-way down the lousy thing before
    I realized, you know – I mean, before I knew it was a Blighty
    fag . . . So how was I to feel? . . . What would you have
    done? . . . You tell me, Bammo . . . I could have choked,
    you know . . . I've got a brother who's up country.

BAMFORTH: If he's dropped in with a gang of Nips who
    think like you, God help the kiddie. God help him!

MACLEISH: I thought he'd looted them!

BAMFORTH: And so you pull the big brave hero bull. The
    raving highlander. Aren't you the boy? So what you waiting
    for? Well, come on, Jock, finish off the job! (BAMFORTH
    grabs THE PRISONER, *pinning his arms, and swings him*
    round, holding him towards MACLEISH.) Come on, come on!

Come on, he's waiting for the hump. Let's see you slot him, Jock! Drop him one on! Let's see you do your stuff! Smash his face for him! Drop him one on!

MACLEISH: Lay off it, Bamforth.

MITCHEM: O.K., Bamforth, jack it in.

BAMFORTH: Haven't any of you got the guts to go the bundle? You were snapping at the leash when I walked in. What about you, Taff? You want to have a crack at him?

MITCHEM: I said, drop it.

BAMFORTH (*loosing his hold on* THE PRISONER): I didn't start it.

THE PRISONER *sits on form and returns the articles to his trouser pockets.*

EVANS: It was a mistake, Bammo.

BAMFORTH: You bet it was.

EVANS: We thought he'd whipped them.

BAMFORTH (*stoops and picks up the wallet and a piece of the torn photographs*): You bastards. You even had to rip his pictures up. You couldn't leave him them even!

EVANS: I'll give you a hand to pick them up.

BAMFORTH: You couldn't even leave him them!

EVANS (*bends down and collects the torn pieces of the photographs*): Happen he can stick them together again, Bammo. Here's a bit with a head on it. He could stick them together, easy enough, with a pot of paste and a brush.

BAMFORTH: Aw . . . Dry up, you Welsh burk.

EVANS (*rises and crosses to* THE PRISONER): Tojo . . . Tojo, boy. (THE PRISONER *looks up.*) I got your pieces for you. You can stick them together again. Pot of paste and a bit of fiddling and they'll be right as rain. (MITCHEM *and* MACLEISH *move away from* THE PRISONER.) Good as ever they was . . . Well, not quite as good, happen, but if you don't mind the joins and do them careful it won't matter, will it? (EVANS *holds out the torn pieces, but* THE PRISONER, *fearing further blows, is hesitant in accepting them.*) Go on, Tojo son, you have them back. Better than nothing, anyway. (THE PRISONER *takes the torn fragments and examines them one by one.*) Some of them are only torn in two. All the face is there on that one. (THE PRISONER *continues to examine the pieces.* EVANS *stoops to retrieve a scrap of a photograph which he had overlooked previously.*) A bit here I missed. Looks like a little bit of a little bit of a girlie. (*He examines the fragment closely.*) Oh no, it's a boy, is that. (*He presses the scrap into the hands of* THE PRISONER.) You'll . . . you'll be needing that as well.

BAMFORTH (*handing the wallet to* EVANS): Here, Taff, stick him this.

EVANS: Right, boyo. (*He hands the wallet to* THE PRISONER.) And here's your wallet, Tojo boy.

MACLEISH (*picks up the cigarette case from the floor and gives it to* BAMFORTH): He'd better have this back too. He'll . . . Maybe he'll be feeling in need of a smoke.

BAMFORTH: Yeh . . . Thanks, Jock. (*He crosses to return the cigarette case.*)

JOHNSTONE: Bamforth! Just a minute, lad.

BAMFORTH: Yeh?

JOHNSTONE: I'd like a look at that before you hand it on to him.

BAMFORTH: Ask him. Not me. It's his.

JOHNSTONE: He'll get it back. I only want it for a minute.

BAMFORTH (*hesitates, then crosses and hands the case to* JOHNSTONE): He'd better get it back.

JOHNSTONE: He will. (*He inspects the case, slowly turning it over in his hands, then tosses it to* BAMFORTH. BAMFORTH *crosses to return it to* THE PRISONER.) Bamforth!

BAMFORTH (*turns*): You want something else?

JOHNSTONE: No, lad. Nothing. I was just wondering, that's all.

BAMFORTH: Well?

JOHNSTONE: Are you feeling in a generous mood to-day?

BAMFORTH: What's that supposed to signify?

JOHNSTONE: Did you give him the case as well?

BAMFORTH: I gave him half a dozen fags, that's all. I haven't got a case myself to give away. I gave him half a dozen snouts, I've told you half a dozen times. The case belongs to him.

JOHNSTONE: Does it?

BAMFORTH: The case is his.

JOHNSTONE: That's interesting. You'd better have another shufti at it, then.

   BAMFORTH *inspects the case and is about to return it to* THE PRISONER.

MITCHEM: Pass it over, Bamforth.

BAMFORTH: What for? It's his.

MITCHEM: I'd like to once it over for myself.

BAMFORTH (*tosses the case to* MITCHEM, *who also examines it, then turns his glance upon* THE PRISONER): All right! So it's a British case!

JOHNSTONE: Made in Birmingham.

BAMFORTH: So what? What's that supposed to prove?

MITCHEM: So tell us now how he got hold of it.

BAMFORTH: I don't know. Don't ask me.

JOHNSTONE: I bloody do! The way he got the snouts.

BAMFORTH: I gave him the fags.

JOHNSTONE: So you say.

BAMFORTH: I gave him the fags!

MITCHEM: And what about the case?

BAMFORTH: Look – I don't know. I've told you – I don't know.

EVANS: So he has been on the lifting lark? Half-inching from the boys up country.

MACLEISH: It begins to look that way.

   MACLEISH *and* EVANS *move menacingly towards* THE PRISONER.

BAMFORTH (*planting himself between* THE PRISONER *and*

EVANS *and* MACLEISH): You've got it all sorted out between you.

EVANS: It stands to reason, man.

BAMFORTH: You ought to be in Scotland Yard, you lads. In Security.

MACLEISH: It's pretty obvious he's pinched the thing.

BAMFORTH: Is it?

EVANS: How else could he have got it, Bammo?

BAMFORTH: You pair of ignorant crones! Sherlock-Taffy-Bloody-Holmes and Charlie MacChan. Sexy Blake and his tartan boy assistant. How do I know where he got it from? It's you bright pair who seem to know the answers. You tell me. If I were you I'd have it cased for bloodstains and fingerprints with a magnifying glass. How does anybody cop on to a fag case? Eh? You buy them! In shops! With money! You know what money is, eh? Money, you know. The stuff they give you on a Friday night. Bits of paper. and little round rings. That's the carry-on in my home town. Where you come from they still swop things for sheep.

MACLEISH: It's a British case, Bamforth.

BAMFORTH: You're a head case, Jock. I've got a little skin and blister back in Blighty. Twelve years old. She carts around a squinting Nippo doll. Know how she got it? One night, instead of being tucked up in her little bed, she was out roaming the streets with a chopper. She knocked off nine Nippo nippers in a night nursery and nicked a golliwog, two teddy-bears and this here doll. You want to know how we found out? It's got 'Made in Japan' stamped across its pink behind. Now, work that one out.

MITCHEM: It won't wash, Bamforth. The Nips don't import fancy swag. They churn it out themselves and flog it abroad.

BAMFORTH (*stepping aside to give* MACLEISH *and* EVANS *access to* THE PRISONER): All right! Go on. Beat him up, then. Work him over. Enjoy yourselves for once. Have a good time. Look – listen. You want to know something? You want to know who's got the biggest hoard of loot in the Far East, bar none? Who's collected more Jap swag than any regiment? I'll introduce him. (BAMFORTH *crosses to rear of hut and raises Whitaker's hand.*) On my right and stepping in the ring at six stone six – the terror of the Newcastle Church Army Hostel: Private Winnie Whitaker!

WHITAKER (*embarrassed at being drawn into the proceedings*): Cut it out, Bammo.

BAMFORTH: Take a bow, son. Here he is. The sole proprietor of the Samuel Whitaker War Museum. It's worth hard gelt in anybody's lingo.

   WHITAKER *manages to extricate his hand from Bamforth's grip.*

MITCHEM: What are you getting at?

BAMFORTH: Ask the boy himself. He's the proud possessor. Come on, Whitaker, my old son, don't be bashful. Tell them all about your battle honours. What you did in the war, dad.

WHITAKER: I don't know what you're supposed to be talking about.

BAMFORTH: Don't you? Smudger knows. Smudger's seen it. He can bear me out.

SMITH: Leave the kid alone, Bammo. There's no harm in it.

BAMFORTH: It's true, isn't it?

SMITH: Look – lay off the lad.

BAMFORTH: Is it the truth?

SMITH: Yes . . . He's got a bit of swag.

BAMFORTH: A bit! That's the bloody understatement of the war, is that.

WHITAKER: It's only souvenirs, Bammo.

EVANS: What kind of souvenirs you got, Sammy?

BAMFORTH: He's got it in his locker back at camp. Smudge and me had a shufti one morning when he left it open. Well, come on Whitto, don't be shy. Tell them what you've got.

WHITAKER: Just some odds and ends, man, and a few things I've picked up, that's all.

BAMFORTH: Tell them!

WHITAKER: Some Jap buttons and a couple of rounds.

BAMFORTH: And the rest.

WHITAKER: A nippo cap badge and a belt.

BAMFORTH: Go on.

WHITAKER: That's all.

BAMFORTH: I've seen inside your locker.

WHITAKER: That's all there is.

BAMFORTH: You're lying, Whitaker!

WHITAKER: I'm not, man. I've not got anything else.

BAMFORTH: You're a lying get!

WHITAKER: Only some bits and pieces.

SMITH: Let him alone, Bamforth.

BAMFORTH: His locker's loaded with Jap loot. It's like a little Tokyo inside his locker.

WHITAKER: They're only souvenirs, Bammo.

BAMFORTH: Don't give me that. There's half the emperor's arsenal and the Imperial quartermaster's stores in there. When you get home with that lot, Whitaker, you won't half give the family the bull. Will you be able to chat them up, boy, on how you won the war. The Tyneside hero. (*To* EVANS *and* MACLEISH.) And you lot want to string the fives on Tojo just because he's got a Blighty fag case. If the Nips lay hands on Whitaker they'll work it out that he's a sort of military Al Capone. Him! Whitaker! Whining Whitaker. The boy who has a nervous breakdown at the thought of Madame Butterfly. Show him a rice pudding and he gets the screaming ab–dabs. He's never even seen a Jap excepting that one there.

SMITH: Can't you leave the lad alone.

BAMFORTH: All right. I've done with him. But just for the book, Whitaker, just to put these boys here right – just tell them how you copped on to the spoils of war.

WHITAKER: I don't know. I just . . . they just came into my possession.

BAMFORTH: Tell them how!

WHITAKER: I swopped some things for them. In the N.A.A.F.I. Down the U.J. Club. I swopped them for some stuff I had myself – with some blokes I met who'd come down from up country.

BAMFORTH: That's all I want to know.

WHITAKER: It's not a crime.

BAMFORTH: No. No, it's not a crime. (*Crossing downstage.*) It's not a crime to have a fag case either. Now, go on, Jock, beat up the Nip.

MACLEISH: You still haven't proved, to my satisfaction, that that's the way he got the case.

BAMFORTH: You try and prove it different.

MACLEISH (*turning away from* THE PRISONER): . . . Och, what's it matter anyway . . .

MITCHEM: Evans!

EVANS: Sarge?

MITCHEM (*tossing the cigarette case to* EVANS): You'd better give him this back.

EVANS: Righto.

   EVANS *gives the case to* THE PRISONER, *who opens it, takes out a cigarette and offers one to* EVANS, *who hesitates and then accepts.* EVANS *takes out a box of matches and gives* THE PRISONER *a light.*

WHITAKER (*desiring to change the conversation*): Sergeant Mitchem . . .

MITCHEM: What's your worry?

WHITAKER: I was wondering about the time . . .

MITCHEM: Do you ever do anything else?

WHITAKER: I mean about reliefs. For Smudger and myself. It's well turned half-past now.

MITCHEM: I know! . . . All right. Who's next for stag?

MACLEISH (*collects his rifle and crosses to rear*): Me, for one.

MITCHEM: Take over from Ticker Whitaker before he does his nut.

WHITAKER: I only mentioned it in case it might have slipped your memory, Sarge.

MITCHEM: Tick, tick, tick! You should have been a bloody clock.

WHITAKER (*having been relieved by* MACLEISH, *he crosses downstage*): I wasn't complaining. I thought you'd forgotten.

MITCHEM: I'm not likely to with you around. (*Points to his watch.*) If ever this packs in on me I'll wrap you around my wrist. Evans!

EVANS: Sarge?

MITCHEM: Give Smudge a break. (*Indicating* THE PRISONER.) Bamforth, you just keep an eye on him.

BAMFORTH: He's all right.

MITCHEM: Just keep an eye on him, that's all.

EVANS (*collects his rifle and crosses towards* SMITH. *As he approaches he shoulders his rifle and carries out a 'cod' guard mounting routine with exaggerated smartness.* SMITH *obeys the orders*): Old guard . . . 'shun! Stand at . . . ease! 'Shun! . . . Slope . . . Arms! One – two-three, one – two-three, one! . . . Order . . . arms! One–two-three, one–two-three, one! Very good, Smudger boy. You should have joined the Guards. The sentries will now dismiss for a crafty smoke in the boiler house . . . old guard – to the guard room . . . Dis . . .

JOHNSTONE: All right, Evans. Cut out the funny stuff.

EVANS: You see how it is, Smudger? When you try to be regimental they won't have it. O.K., boyo, you scarper. I'll take over here.

SMITH: It's all yours, Taff.

EVANS *takes up his position at the window as* SMITH *crosses downstage.* WHITAKER *and* SMITH *prop their rifles against the wall.*

WHITAKER: Hey, Taff!

EVANS: What is it, boy?

WHITAKER: Can I have a look at your book? That one you were reading out of earlier on?

EVANS: In my small pack, Whitto.

WHITAKER (*crossing to take magazine from Evans's pack which is on the form by* THE PRISONER): Thanks, Taffy.

BAMFORTH (*as* WHITAKER *gives* THE PRISONER *a wide berth*): It's all right, Whitto, he won't bite you, son. (BAMFORTH *watches* WHITAKER *as he takes the magazine from the pack and settles himself on the extreme end of the form.*) You trying to improve your mind?

WHITAKER: I just wanted to pass a few minutes on. (*He flicks through the pages.*) Where's that story that Taff was telling us about? The one with the Arabs.

SMITH: It's a serial, Sammy. No good starting that.

WHITAKER: I don't mind. It's something to read.

BAMFORTH: You screw the pictures, Whitaker. No good stuffing your head up with them long words. Have a butcher's at the corset adverts on the last page.

SMITH: He's not old enough for them.

BAMFORTH: He's got to start sometime. He can't stay ignorant for ever.

WHITAKER: Who's ignorant?

BAMFORTH: You are! Ignorant as a pig. Pig-ignorant, boy, that's you.

WHITAKER: That's all you know, Bamforth.

BAMFORTH: Hark at him! The innocent abroad. The voice of experience. They lock their daughters up in Newcastle when he's on leave. Go on, Whitaker, you've never been with a bint in your life.

WHITAKER: That just shows how much you know, boy!

SMITH: Never mind him, Sammy. He's pulling your leg.

WHITAKER: He doesn't know so much himself.

BAMFORTH: Have you ever been with a woman, Whitaker?

WHITAKER: 'Course I have. I was courting when I left Blighty.

BAMFORTH: I bet.

SMITH: Newcastle girl, Sammy?

WHITAKER: No. Darlington lass. I met her at a dance once when I was stationed at Catterick.

BAMFORTH: Dancing! Get him! He'll be drinking beer and playing cards for money next.

WHITAKER: It was in a church hall – the dance, I mean. One of the lads in the billet took me. That's how I met this girl.

SMITH: Got a photograph?

WHITAKER: I've got a couple back at camp.

SMITH: What's she like? Bramah, eh?

WHITAKER: She's . . . well, she's sort of pretty, you know, like. Mary. That's her name. Mary Pearson. Comes up to about my shoulder and sort of yellowish hair. Works for an insurance company. In the office. Oh, she's . . . she's bloody pretty, Smudge. Nothing outstanding, like – but, boy, she's pretty. We was courting for three months very nearly. I was up there doing my basic training.

SMITH: Take her out much, did you?

WHITAKER: I used to get to meet her a couple of times a week, like. Whenever I could skive off. Get the bus from camp centre into Darlington and meet her nights outside a shop. Some nights we'd go to the pictures – or dancing – or something – when I could afford it, like. I wasn't loaded them days. So most nights we'd just walk up through the park, you know. Along by the river. The middle of summer I was at Catterick. Was it hot then, boy! Oh, man . . .! She's only seventeen just – is it a bit young, do you think?

SMITH: Doesn't seem to make much difference – these days.

WHITAKER: So we'd just walk along by the side of the river, like. Up as far as the bridge. Happen sit down and watch them playing bowls. Sit for ten minutes or so, get up and walk back. Just a steady stroll, you know. I never

had much money – only my bus fare there and back sometimes – but it was . . . Oh, boy! Oh, you know – we had
some smashing times together me and her. I wish I was
back there now, boy.

SMITH: Write to her, do you?

WHITAKER: When I get the chance. When I'm back in
camp. Every day if I've got the time.

SMITH: Roll on the duration, eh?

WHITAKER: I used to hear from her twice a week. I haven't
had a letter for over a month. Almost six weeks.

SMITH: You know how it is, Sammy. Maybe she's busy.

WHITAKER: I don't know. I'm thinking happen she's got
fixed up with another bloke.

SMITH: Maybe the mail's been held up.

WHITAKER: I get plenty from my mother and the old man.
I think it's another bloke she's with.

SMITH: You don't want to think like that.

WHITAKER: The letters – the writing – things she said – it
was different. Towards the last one, like.

SMITH: Happen be one waiting for you when you get back
tomorrow.

WHITAKER: Aye. Happen so . . . I don't know. I've sort of,
given up, like. Hoping, you know.

*It is early evening and the light has begun to dim. The jungle
is silent and a stillness falls upon the patrol.* BAMFORTH *begins
to sing – quietly and with a touch of sadness.*

BAMFORTH: A handsome young private lay dying,
        At the edge of the jungle he lay.
        The Regiment gathered round him,
        To hear for the last words he'd say.
        'Take the trigger-guard out of my kidneys,
        Take the magazine out of my brain,
        Take the barrel from out of my back-bone,
        And assemble my rifle again . . .'

(In an attempt to restore the previous mood, BAMFORTH *rubs*

the top of the Prisoner's head playfully.) Now then, Tojo, my old flowerpot, what did you think of that? That's better than you cop on from the Tokyo geisha fillies.

EVANS (*turning at window*): It'll not be long before it's dark now, Sarge.

MACLEISH (*without turning from window*): It's quiet out there. It's bloody quiet.

MITCHEM (*rising*): Time we got ready for the push then. Got packed up. Got things – sorted out.

BAMFORTH (*having taken a swig from his water bottle, he wipes the lip and offers the bottle to* THE PRISONER): Come on, Tojo son. Get a gob of this before we go.

THE PRISONER *accepts the bottle gratefully.*

JOHNSTONE: There's no more buckshees for the Nippo, Bamforth.

THE PRISONER, *sensing the meaning from Johnstone's tone, returns the water bottle to* BAMFORTH *without drinking.*

BAMFORTH (*puts down the water bottle and turns to face* JOHN-STONE): I've warned you, Johnno. Don't overstep them tapes. I'll not take any more of the patter. Is it O.K. if I give the prisoner a drink, Sarge?

MITCHEM: You heard what Corporal Johnstone said, Bamforth.

BAMFORTH (*incredulous*): You what?

JOHNSTONE: There's no more water for the Nippo.

BAMFORTH: Like Hell there isn't. The bloke's got to drink.

MITCHEM: He's had a drink – earlier on this afternoon. I gave him one myself.

BAMFORTH: He's not a camel!

MITCHEM: I'm sorry, Bamforth. We've none to spare for him.

BAMFORTH: Sorry!

MITCHEM: We'll need every drop we've got for getting back. It's dead certain that there'll be a gang of Nips round every water hole from here to base.

BAMFORTH: So we share out what we've got.

MITCHEM: No.

BAMFORTH: He gets half of mine.

MITCHEM: No! There's none for him.

BAMFORTH: He'll have to have a drink sometime. He can't go the distance without – you've got to get him back as well. (*He waits for a reply.*) We're taking him as well!

MITCHEM: I'm sorry.

JOHNSTONE: He's stopping where he is. (*He picks up the Prisoner's bayonet from the table.*) It's cobbler's for him.

BAMFORTH: No.

MITCHEM: I've got no choice.

BAMFORTH: You said he was going back.

MITCHEM: He was – before. The circumstances are altered. The situation's changed. I can't take him along.

BAMFORTH: What's the poor get done to us?

MITCHEM: It's a war. It's something in a uniform and it's a different shade to mine.

BAMFORTH (*positioning himself between* THE PRISONER *and* JOHNSTONE): You're not doing it, Johnno.

JOHNSTONE: You laying odds on that?

BAMFORTH: For Christ's sake!

JOHNSTONE: It's a bloody Nip.

BAMFORTH: He's a man!

JOHNSTONE (*crossing a few paces towards* THE PRISONER): Shift yourself, Bamforth. Get out of the way.

BAMFORTH: You're not doing it.

MITCHEM: Bamforth, shift yourself.

BAMFORTH: You're a bastard, Mitchem.

MITCHEM: I wish to God I was.

BAMFORTH: You're a dirty bastard, Mitchem.

MITCHEM: As far as I'm concerned, it's all these lads or him.

BAMFORTH: It's him and me.

MITCHEM (*crossing to join* JOHNSTONE): Get to one side. That's an order.

BAMFORTH: Stick it.

MITCHEM: For the last time, Bamforth, move over.

BAMFORTH: Try moving me.

MITCHEM: I've not got time to mess about.

BAMFORTH: So come on, Whitaker! Don't sit there, lad. Who's side you on? (WHITAKER *rises slowly from the form. For a moment it would seem that he is going to stand by* BAMFORTH *but he crosses the room to stand beyond* MITCHEM *and* JOHNSTONE.) You've got no guts, Whitaker. You know that, boy? You've just got no guts.

WHITAKER: We've got to get back, Bammo.

BAMFORTH: You're a gutless slob!

WHITAKER: I've got to get back!

BAMFORTH: Evans. Taffy, Taff! (EVANS *turns from the window*): Put the gun on these two, son.

EVANS: I reckon Mitch is right, you know. We couldn't get him back to camp, could we, boyo? The Nips must have a Div between the camp and us.

BAMFORTH: He's going to kill him, you nit!

EVANS: You never know about that fag case, do you, son?

BAMFORTH: What's the fag case got to do with it! . . . Smudger! Smudger, now it's up to you.

SMITH: Don't ask me, Bammo. Leave me out of it.

BAMFORTH: You're in it, Smudge. You're in it up to here.

SMITH: I just take orders. I just do as I'm told. I just plod on.

BAMFORTH: The plodding on has stopped. Right here. Right here you stop and make a stand. He's got a wife and kids.

SMITH: I've got a wife and kids myself. Drop it, Bammo, it's like Mitch says – it's him or us.

BAMFORTH: Jock! . . . Jock! (MACLEISH *continues to stare out of the window.*) Macleish! . . . (MACLEISH *does not move.*) I hope they carve your brother up. Get that? I hope they carve your bloody brother up!

MITCHEM: All right, Bamforth, you've had your say. Now shift.

BAMFORTH: Shift me! Come on, heroes, shift me!

MITCHEM: Whitaker! Grab a gun and cover the Nip.

BAMFORTH: Don't do it, Whitaker. Stay out of it.

MITCHEM: Whitaker!

> WHITAKER *picks up a sten from the table and crosses to cover* THE PRISONER, *who has realized the implications and is trembling with fear.* MITCHEM *and* JOHNSTONE *move forward to overpower* BAMFORTH. JOHNSTONE *drops the bayonet on the floor and, together with* MITCHEM, *grapples with* BAMFORTH. *As they fight* THE PRISONER *begins to rise to his feet.*

WHITAKER (*already in a state of fear himself*): Get down! . . . Sit down! . . . (THE PRISONER *continues to rise.*) Sit down, you stupid man, or I'll have to put a bullet into you . . . THE PRISONER *is standing upright as Whitaker's finger tightens on the trigger. A long burst from the sten shudders the hut and the bullets slam home into the body of the Prisoner like hammer blows.* THE PRISONER *doubles up and falls to the floor. The fight stops. There is a pause.* WHITAKER *drops the sten and buries his face in his hands.*) God . . . God . . . God . . . (*His voice swells.*) Oh, God!

MITCHEM: Well, that should roust out every Nip from here to Tokyo. You've made a mess of that, lad. (WHITAKER, *uncomprehending, looks at his hands.* MITCHEM *seizes him by the shoulders and shakes him savagely.*) Come on, come on! Come out of it! He's just the first.

BAMFORTH: You've got the biggest souvenir of all. You've done it this time, Whitaker. Take that and hang it on the front room wall . . .

> *Bamforth's words are cut short as* MITCHEM *strikes him across the face.*

MITCHEM: We've had enough from you.

> EVANS *and* MACLEISH *have left their posts and, together with* SMITH, *are drawn in fascination towards the body of the Prisoner.*

JOHNSTONE: All right. Get back. It's just a corpse. You'll see a whole lot more like that before you've done.

MITCHEM: Right. All of you. We've moving out. In double time. Get your gear together. Thirty seconds and we're off. Any longer and this place will be rotten with Nips. Any man not ready stays behind. Move!

The members of the patrol put on their packs, ammunition pouches, etc.

MITCHEM: Johnno, ditch your stuff. Can you work the set? (JOHNSTONE *nods assent and crosses to radio.*) Give it one last crack. (JOHNSTONE *switches on the set and the crackle of interference grows behind.*) We haven't got a snowball's chance in Hell of getting back. So try and let them know the Japs have broken through.

JOHNSTONE (*nods and switches to 'transmit'*): Blue Patrol calling Red Leader . . . Blue Patrol calling Red Leader . . . Are you receiving me . . . Are you receiving me . . . Come in Red Leader . . . Over . . . (JOHNSTONE *switches to 'receive' and the interference swells.*) Not a rotten peep.

MITCHEM: All right. Jack it in.

JOHNSTONE (*rips off headphones, leaving the set switched on. He straps on his ammunition pouches and picks up the sten from the floor.*) Let's have you then! We're pushing off!

MITCHEM (*picking up his own sten*): Leave what you haven't got. And move!

The members of the patrol collect their rifles and cross to the door. JOHNSTONE *glances out of the window.*

JOHNSTONE: All clear.

MITCHEM (*opens the door*): I'll break the trail. Johnno, you bring up the rear. (JOHNSTONE *nods.*) All right, let's go.

One by one the members of the patrol follow MITCHEM *through the door.* JOHNSTONE *is the last to leave. As the door closes behind* JOHNSTONE *the interference increases on the set and suddenly it bursts into life.*

OPERATOR (*on distort*): . . . Red Leader calling Blue Patrol

... Red Leader calling Blue Patrol ... Come in Blue Patrol
... Over ...

*A machine-gun chatters in the jungle and is joined by another.
We hear the sound of one or two rifles and the screams of dying
men. The noise of gunfire fades away, to leave only the whimper
of one wounded man—it is* WHITAKER. *The door is pushed open
and* JOHNSTONE *enters. He has a bullet wound in his side and
the blood is seeping through his shirt. Slamming the door shut,
he leans upon it to regain his breath.*

WHITAKER (*screams out from the jungle in fear*): God! ... God!
... (*A final cry of terror louder than any we have heard previously.*)
Mother ... !

We hear the sound of a single shot and WHITAKER *is dead.*
JOHNSTONE *presses his hand to his side. The set splutters into
life again.*

OPERATOR (*on distort*): ... Are you receiving me, Blue
Patrol? ... Are you receiving me? ... Over ...

JOHNSTONE (*crosses slowly to the set, picks up hand-set and
switches to 'transmit'*): Get knotted! All of you! You hear?
The whole damn lot of you!

*JOHNSTONE switches off the set and crosses towards the body
of the Prisoner. As he passes the window there is a short
burst of machine-gun fire. He ducks below window level. Squatting
by the side of the body, he takes the cigarette case from the Prisoner's
pocket and helps himself to a cigarette. Sticking the cigarette in
his mouth, he returns the case to the Prisoner's pocket. He tugs
the white silk scarf, now spattered with blood, from the Prisoner's
neck and crawls across to beneath the window, where he ties the
scarf round the barrel of his sten. It has all required a great effort,
and he lights the cigarette and inhales deeply before continuing.
Squatting below the window, he waves the white flag and, in
turn, takes long pulls at the cigarette. For a moment there is com-
plete silence and then a bird sings out in the jungle.*

THE CURTAIN FALLS

GLOSSARY OF LESS COMMON SLANG AND REFERENCES

(Meanings are given with reference to use on the pages shown)

Ab-dabs, usually *screaming*, 21, 44: hysterical fit, 75: bowel upset

Al Capone, 75: American gangster

Barrack-room lawyer, 26: man who makes trouble by insisting on legal rights

Batt., 28: battery

Blighty, 14, 25, 52, 56, 66, 69, 73, 75, 79: England, English (from Hindustani *bilayati*)

Blocks, put the blocks on, 48: stop

Bog, 8: latrine

Book, 26, 60: rigid adherence to what is legal, i.e. in the book of King's Regulations

Bramah, 79: gorgeously beautiful (from Hindu deity, whose idols were so)

Buckshee, 81: gift, 32: free, hence worthless (from Persian word for present)

Bull, 15, 55, 57, 69, 75: nonsense, empty talk

Bundle, go a bundle on, 20, 56, 70: be wildly enthusiastic about or stake everything on, make a bold bid

Bungy, 18: food

Butcher's, 78: look (rhyming slang, *butcher's hook*)

Butterfly, Madame, 75: i.e. anything Japanese (Madame Butterfly is the Japanese heroine of Puccini's opera of that name)

Call out the time, 21, 32, 46: talk loudly and confidently, 21: give orders

Cap and belt off, 22: military practice of taking off a soldier's hat and belt before parading him for disciplinary sentence

Carve up (v), 5: beat up, 83: kill; (n), 14: swindle

Case (v), 73: examine

Charlie MacChan, 73: Charlie Chan was a detective in a series of films. A *Charlie* (56) is a fool (possibly from Charlie Chaplin)

Chuff, 29: disregard, 32: curse

Civvy street, 5: civilian life

Cobbler's, 82: end (in Australia the last sheep to be sheared is called the cobbler's – originally perhaps the *cobbler's last*)

Cod, 20, 77: mock

Come: assert, insist on, 23: *Come the regimental*, 10: insist on procedure according to King's Regulations. *Come the hard case stuff*, 25: try to appear tough. *Come his rank:* assert his authority. *Come the greater glory of mankind*, 60: claim to care greatly about ideals. *Comes the ab-dabs*, 44: goes berserk

Come it on, 5, 21, 25, 26, 40, 43: behave provocatively, ask for trouble

Compo, 4: composition pack containing rations for one day

Connor, 66: food (from Urdu *Khana*)

Conshi, 60: conscientious objector to fighting

Cop, 37, 39, 57, 61: Get, take. *Cop on to, cop on for, cop on*, 40, 43, 56, 61, 73, 75: get, accept, get possession of, get involved with. *No cop*, 57: no use

Creamer, 14: mug (rhyming slang – cream-jug)

Creek, 31, 32, 41: *up the creek without a paddle*: 3, 13: in difficulties (from navy slang – away from anchorage)

Creep (n), 5, 40: contemptible person; (v), 10: curry favour, sneak

Crumb (n), 32: contemptible person; (adj), 18: contemptible (also *crummy*)

Dancers, 56: stairs

Detail, 18, 43: party detailed or ordered to do a particular duty

Dinky-doo, number-two, 45: rhyme for 2 in games like Housie-housie (in Australia *dinkum* means good)

Dis, 3, 9, 28: out of order (especially of radio equipment)

Div., 83: division, military unit organized under single command and capable of operating independently. An infantry division would include roughly 12,000 men.

Do, do in, or *do for*, 36, 42, 59, 60: kill

Doolally, 9: weak, defective (from Deolali, mental hospital in India)

Dracula, 55: bloodsucking monster, familiar in horror films

Drag, 4, 34: brief smoke

Drop (you) one on, 7, 70: hit (you)

Drum, 15: house, lodging

Duff, 29: useless, defective

Fives, 75: fists

Fix (n), *get a fix on*, 49: locate, get indication of position (service jargon)

Fred Karno's mob, 10, 31: Fred Karno was a pre-1914 comedian, whose performance depicted imbecile incompetence; a wryly satirical soldiers' song of the 1914–18 war began: 'We are Fred Karno's army'

Geisha girls, 30, *Geisha fillies*, 81: Japanese dancing-girls

Gelt, 74: money (from German *geld*)

Geneva Convention, 39: International agreement of 1906 regulating treatment of prisoners of war

Get (n), 22, 34, 40, 75, 82: person, wretch (coarse or abusive term)

Get fell in, 23: order to stand in drill formation (consciously rough and ungrammatical language)

Gillo, 2: move quickly

Ginks, 32: men (coarse term)

Give us the heels together, 10: order us to stand at attention

Gob, 53, 81: drink (*Gob* is originally a dialect word for *mouth*)

Graft, 48: hard work

Gripe, 32: complain

Haggis, 20: peculiarly Scottish dish. Bamforth pulls a Scotsman's leg about haggis, and a Welshman's about leeks or Eisteddfods, in a sort of pointless badinage

Haircut to breakfast time, 5: i.e. at all hours – one version of a phrase commonly used in the Services

Half-inch, 52, 72: steal (rhyming with *pinch*)

Happen, 54, 57, 61, 65, 67, 70, 79, 80: perhaps (from Northern dialect)

Hard case, 25, 26: tough, aggressive person

Harry, 32, 53, 56, 59: name used disparagingly. Harry Tate was a comedian, and Harry Tate's army was similar to Fred Karno's mob

Henry Hall, 9: former conductor of BBC dance orchestra

How's your father?, 14: music-hall catchphrase, here used without precise meaning but with indefinable comic suggestion, cf., *Haircut to breakfast time*

Hump (n), 36, 70: effort, force, blow. (v), 18: carry. *Gets my hump*, 67: annoys. *Humpy*, 4: load

i.c., 4, 9, 10: in charge

Jack it in, 5, 38, 45, 70, 85: stop it, give it up, 54: abandon fighting

Jack the Ripper, 37: 19th century murderer

Joskins, 32: very raw recruits

Joy, 28: success, satisfaction

Judies, 14, 56: girls

Kick-off, 13: start

King's Regs, 23, 26: King's Regulations lay down the soldier's duties, rights and procedures. *To come King's Regs* is to insist on legal rights or obligations

Kip, 4, 29: sleep

Knock off, 17: stop; 43: kill; 52: steal

Knotted, Get knotted: 20, 86: coarse insult (The offensiveness depends on context, not meaning)

Kybosh, put the: 48 stop, thwart

Lacas, 2: anglicized version of Malay word *lêcas* meaning *hurry up!*

Looey, 11: lieutenant

Meal, Don't make a meal out of it, 41: don't overdo it

Mob, 18, 25, 27, 48, 59: military unit

Mockers, 39; *put the mockers on* (cockney): put the evil eye on, i.e. kill

Mouth, 2: insolence; *big with the mouth*, 23: talking aggressively; *shoot off your mouth*, 31: talk big

Muckers, 44: pals (men who *muck in together*)

Mugs away, 56: phrase used in the game of darts, meaning that the losers of the last game are to start the next. Mitchem puns on this special sense of 'mugs' and the more common meaning (dupes or simpletons)

N.A.A.F.I., 18, 52, 76: canteen run by Navy, Army and Air Forces Institutes

Nick (n), 3: prison; (v), 73: steal

Nip, Nippo, 20, 23, 27, 32, *et passim*: Japanese

Nub, 35: cigarette end; 68: cigarette

Nut, do his nut, 8, 32: get excited or angry; 61: go berserk

Nut, put in the, 5: butt an opponent with the head

Once over, 72: look at

Orders, 22: *warning you for C.O.'s orders*: threatening to bring you before the Commanding Officer for breach of discipline

P.B.I., 19: poor bloody infantry

Press, up to, 34: up to the present moment

Pull, 69: assert, plead, use influence of, *pull his rank*, 6, *pull the tape*, 21

Put him one on, 23: aim a blow at him

Rising Sun, 20: emblem of Japan

Rita Hayworth, 38: film star

Roll on, 29, 53; *Roll on the Duration*, 80: was a common expression of exasperation with the war, a wry appeal for the end of it

Rookie, xxi, xxii: raw beginner (apparently from recruit)

R.S.M., 53: Regimental Sergeant-Major, responsible for discipline

Sarge, 4, 27, 28, *et passim*: abbreviation of *sergeant* as form of address, familiar or even friendly in tone

Sarnt, 24, 25, 26, *et passim*: smart, soldierly form of *sergeant*, intended to be respectful or mock-respectful

Saw you coming, they, 51: they realised you were easily duped

Say that again, you can, 61: too true! Glum or ironic exclamation of agreement

Scarper, 19, 77: abscond, escape (Italian *scappare*. Also punning association with rhyming slang, *Scapa Flow* for *go*)

Screaming ab-dabs: see *ab-dabs*

Screw, 78: same idea as *chuff*, but ruder.

Sew up, 48: deal with a problem

Shouting the odds, 6: talking loudly and importantly

Shufti, 66, 72, 74: look (from Arabic)

Skin and blister, 73: rhyming slang for *sister*

Skive, 26, 34: escape duty

Slot, 70: stab

Snappers, 15, 45: children

Snout, 69, 72: cigarette

S.O.B., 28: son of a bitch (American insult)

Sort out, 5, 22: quarrel by fighting; 14: deal with 81: organise

Spout, 31: breech (of rifles)

Stag, 2, 3, 27, 39, 76: sentry duty

Stick, 19, 67, 83: treat contemptuously, dispose of

Stick, make it, 46: sustain, get (e.g. a charge) proved and acted on

Stripes, three, 26: chevron of sergeant's rank

Stroll on, 11, 14, 18, 19, 21, 31, 45: variant of *roll on*, q.v.

Swallow, 35: short smoke

Tapes, 5, 7, 10, 21, 22, 60, 61: N.C.O.'s stripes indicating rank. *Over-step them tapes*, 81: exceed your authority

Tick, 27, 77: complaint

Tod, on one's, 12, 20, 34, 35: alone (from rhyming slang: *on his Tod Sloan, on his own*)

Toe-rag, 5: despicable person who licks the sergeant's boots

Tojo, 20, 30, 37, 40, 42, 43, *et passim*: Japanese Prime Minister, 1941–44

Tripes, 24: entrails

Two's up, 11, 12: (I'm) next in turn

u/s, 3, 28: unserviceable, out of order

U.J. club, 76: Union Jack club for servicemen

Valentino, Rudolph, 57: (1895–1926) star of silent films, famous for 'handsome lover' roles

W.O.Is, xxi: Warrant Officers, first class

Work over, 73: beat up

Yellow peril, 21: supposed threat from Japanese (or Chinese)

Yob, 61: lout (backslang for *boy*)